355.45(5-011) £4-69

78586

The U.S. Military Presence in the Middle East: Problems and Prospects

①

R Adm

Robert J. Hanks

(**Foreign Policy Report**
December 1982)

INSTITUTE FOR FOREIGN POLICY ANALYSIS, INC.
Cambridge, Massachusetts, and Washington, D.C.

Requests for copies of IFPA Foreign Policy Reports should be addressed to the Circulation Manager, Foreign Policy Reports, Institute for Foreign Policy Analysis, Inc., Central Plaza Building, Tenth Floor, 675 Massachusetts Avenue, Cambridge, Massachusetts 02139. (Telephone: 617-492-2116) Please send a check or money order for the correct amount along with your order.

Standing orders for all Foreign Policy Reports will be accepted by the Circulation Manager. Standing order subscribers will automatically receive all future Reports as soon as they are published. Each Report will be accompanied by an invoice.

IFPA also maintains a **mailing list** of individuals and institutions who are notified periodically of new Institute publications. Those desiring to be placed on this list should write to the Circulation Manager, Foreign Policy Reports, at the above address.

The Institute for Foreign Policy Analysis, Inc., incorporated in the Commonwealth of Massachusetts, is a tax-exempt organization under Section 501(c)(3) of the U.S. Internal Revenue Code, and has been granted status as a publicly-supported, nonprivate organization under Section 509(a)(1). Contributions to the Institute are tax-deductible.

Price: $7.50

Library of Congress Catalog Card Number: 82-84308
ISBN 0-89549-047-1

First Printing
Printed by Corporate Press, Inc., Washington, D.C.

Contents

Summary Overview

Since American entry into World War II, the United States has continuously maintained some sort of military presence in and around the Middle East. Commencing with joint allied efforts to provide weaponry and logistics support for use by the hard-pressed troops of the USSR, that posture has varied from time to time as the tides of crisis and conflict ebbed and flowed throughout the region. Whether concerned about the security of the state of Israel, implied threats to the flow of Middle East oil, the seizure of the U.S. Embassy in Teheran in the wake of the Shah's downfall, or the savage Soviet invasion of Afghanistan—the Middle East, particularly that portion lying beyond Suez, has persistently clamored for Washington's attention.

A major problem associated with the Middle East has been the exceedingly varied and, at times, frustratingly ambiguous perils which surface whenever U.S. national interests are at stake. In this connection, the issue of the utility inherent in a "military presence" has always permeated national security calculations. Today, such a display is a far cry from the traditional "gunboat diplomacy" which earned a very bad name in nineteenth-century China. A form of political coercion utilized by every major world power, including the USSR, the military presence is a fact of modern international life, and its anatomy must be thoroughly understood if it is to be effectively employed.

Complicating the problem of maintaining relevant military forces in the Indian Ocean, 12,000 miles from the continental United States, is a dearth of proper bases from which those forward-deployed elements can operate on a sustained basis. Moreover, American difficulties are further compounded by the proximity of powerful Soviet armed forces which can be brought to bear on relatively short notice. Finally, personnel shortages stemming from adoption of the all-volunteer concept of military service in the United States have substantially diminished this nation's military power.

In a belated attempt to rectify this altogether bleak situation in the Middle East, the Carter Administration founded the Rapid Deployment Force (RDF). Both in concept and in fact, it leaves much to be desired, although three years have passed since its inception. Many of the initial shortcomings of the RDF are no nearer to solution today than they were at the time of its establishment.

In the meantime, the collapse of U.S. strategy in the Middle East has further exacerbated the overall situation. Commencing with the fall of the Shah, what had seemed a promising American foreign policy for the

Persian Gulf steadily deteriorated. Through all of this, American actions with respect to the Arab-Israeli dispute have consistently thwarted efforts to shore up the region against increasing Soviet encroachments. Nor have the attitudes of American allies—European and Japanese—been particulary helpful. The studied reluctance of NATO to undertake any collective action beyond the formal boundaries of the Alliance—established in the entirely different global environment which existed at the time of its founding in 1949—is especially disconcerting in light of the ongoing Soviet menace and expanding Western dependence upon Middle East resources. Nevertheless, this is the unpalatable reality which currently confronts U.S. national security planners.

The advent of the Reagan Administration, with its heavy emphasis on restoring American military power—maritime in particular—portends an improved future capability for this nation to safeguard its interests in the Middle East. However, given the long lead-times associated with the production of modern weapons systems, as well as the training of personnel to operate them, it will still be a long time until this capability is on line. Moreover, the time available might be extremely short.

The North Atlantic Treaty Organization and its parent body, the North Atlantic Alliance, still constitute the linchpin of Western security. As such, both groups must be preserved. Nevertheless, the persistent refusal of most West European nations to undertake any collective action to strengthen the defenses of NATO-Europe or to protect common interests beyond the initially defined frontiers of the Alliance, strongly suggests that the American commitment to the common defense should be restructured. Similar imperatives are operative insofar as Japan is concerned. Moreover, the bars to restoring the American strategic position in the region east of Suez, bars which have been erected by historic U.S. policies in the marathon Arab-Israeli confrontation, must be removed.

It is vital that future U.S. diplomatic initiatives impress the foregoing facts on this nation's friends and allies around the globe. Simultaneously, it is equally important that the United States transform its approach to the Arab-Israeli conflict with the objective of eliciting greater cooperation from the moderate states of the Persian Gulf region.

Absent these sorts of changes, the United States will be confronted with a difficult alternative: massive modernizing and expansion of U.S. armed forces. American reliance on overseas resources—fuel and nonfuel—is not likely to decrease. Protecting access to these resources will be a complicated and expensive undertaking. Still the dilemma has to be faced and resolved.

Forward deployments, designed to reduce reaction time to incipient crises and to assure successful outcomes with a minimum of force, are essential. Such a military posture demands enhancement of the quick-reaction capacity of the Marine Corps, a force which can be stationed at sea in areas of most likely need, without the necessity for seeking permission from any other nation.

Similarly, efforts to produce a viable Rapid Deployment Force should be pressed. At the same time, this initiative should be accompanied by a strong effort to form some kind of multilateral entente, probably informal in nature, by means of which the assistance of nations willing to cooperate outside the NATO arena—Great Britain and France particularly—can be enlisted to meet extraregional threats.

Insofar as the restructuring of the U.S.-NATO relationship is concerned, the centerpiece should be the adoption of an essentially maritime national strategy by the United States and a concurrent reduction of this nation's commitment to any major land battle in Central Europe. As a prominent German leader recently said, "The prime error you Americans have made ever since the founding of the North Atlantic Alliance has been in not insisting that the defense of Europe is a European responsibility." This will have to be the case if the United States, given finite limitations on its own military capability, is to protect its own—and the West's—vital interests around the world. This can be done, while still providing significant assistance in the defense of Western Europe and Japan, but only if those nations will accept primary responsibility for their own security.

1.
Introduction

FROM THE American perspective, the most significant change which has taken place in the Middle East during the past two decades has been the strategic transformation occurring in the aftermath of the 1973 Arab-Israeli war. For years, Washington and the American people had routinely indulged themselves in the euphoric belief that they enjoyed absolute energy independence. Despite storm signals flapping on the international horizon and frequent efforts of many far-sighted U.S. observers who perceived the true situation and attempted to broadcast a petroleum alert, Americans persisted in ignoring the facts until reality suddenly confronted them with abrupt and stunning effect in October 1973.

It was the 1973 Arab-Israeli war which brought about the ultimate transformation. Even so, emergence of the strategic importance of these far-away lands was neither then universally recognized nor admitted by the American people. In some instances, it is not acknowledged to this day. The latter fact is illustrated by various perceptions which have continued to be harbored at even the highest levels of recent U.S. Governments. It was, after all, a newly-inaugurated President Jimmy Carter who, in 1977 during the opening weeks of his Administration, proposed that the United States and the Soviet Union agree to complete demilitarization of the entire Indian Ocean region. It should also be noted that it took the brutal Soviet invasion of Afghanistan for this same President, by his own admission, to conclude that the Soviets have not been and are not now as peace-loving and trustworthy as he had previously considered them to be.

Recognition of the increased reliance on Middle East oil—West European and Japanese, as well as American—evolved slowly in the United States and, moreover, is still not complete. It is nonetheless true that the Arab-Israeli war of October 1973 and concurrent Arab wielding of the so-called oil weapon made it abundantly clear to informed analysts that a major international turning point had been reached.

Although the fact of the global energy crunch had not yet fully penetrated the American ken in 1974—when the short-lived Arab embargo was lifted—it gradually did so in the wake of the revolution which overthrew the Shah of Iran and halted production of that nation's nearly six million barrels per day, as well as following the outbreak of the Iran-Iraq war of 1980 when Iraqi exports drastically declined. In both instances, gasoline and home-heating oil shortages immediately appeared in the

1

United States. Even the most obtuse citizen could see that the overly sanguine estimates of American energy independence, to which they had been subjected by the U.S. Government and the American media, were more myth than reality.

In retrospect, one is constrained to observe that the members of OAPEC (the Organization of Arab Petroleum Exporting Countries) really did not do the American people any great favor when they lifted their embargo only five months after imposing it. Once the sanction was removed, the average U.S. citizen promptly went back to doing business at the same old energy stand, and petroleum consumption in the United States began to balloon once more. Had the ban on oil shipments to America been maintained for a longer period—say a year or more—continuing shortages would have convinced most U.S. citizens that the evaluations they had been receiving from their Government and from the media were manifestly wrong; that this nation was no longer energy independent; and, moreover, that urgent efforts would have to be undertaken to conserve oil as well as to search out and develop alternative sources of energy for the future. Today, one can say with a fair degree of certainty that the lifting of the embargo by OAPEC in March 1974 delayed a desperately needed American response to the impending global energy crisis by at least six or seven years. The subject of the so-called oil glut which materialized in 1981 will be subsequently addressed in detail.

Present Western imperatives in the region, while deriving from energy needs, do not, however, stem solely from the 1973 war. There are others which go back much further in time. One of the more important was the 1968 British Labour Government decision to divest itself of the United Kingdom's historic military commitments "East of Suez." That decision, taken in 1968—withdrawal to be completed by the end of 1971—created a military and political power vacuum, particularly in the Persian Gulf. Because of its failure to recognize the rapidly increasing American reliance on oil flowing from the Middle East—particularly that from the Persian Gulf—Washington did not immediately perceive the necessity to fill this power vacuum before it could be exploited by an unfriendly state. It is altogether likely that had the October 1973 war not erupted when it did, U.S. recognition of the strategic importance of the Gulf would have been indefinitely delayed. Equally likely, had an oil embargo not accompanied that war, the resultant strategic neglect would have been still further extended.

Today, few knowledgeable people will contest the fact that the United States, Western Europe and Japan are significantly dependent on Persian Gulf oil. Furthermore, growing numbers of Americans are alarmed by clearly mounting evidence of varied perils endangering continued Western access to that oil. Certainly, the stunning collapse of the Pahlavi dynasty in Iran and subsequent loss of that nation's normal contribution to global petroleum supplies came as a startling and unwelcome surprise. So, too, did the Soviet invasion of Afghanistan, with its ominous portents for the future.

The latter action raised serious questions with respect to Soviet regional designs and turned the world spotlight on Moscow's machinations there and elsewhere around the globe. Particularly in the Persian Gulf, local and international fears arose that the Soviet Union was indeed embarked on a long-predicted campaign to establish dominion over the oil-rich lands of the area, and that the invasion of Afghanistan constituted the opening move in an overt drive to achieve that aim. Governments everywhere closely monitored the continuing chaos in Iran, watching intently for signs of direct Soviet involvement.

The foregoing factors are fundamental to any understanding of the current U.S. military and political posture in the region and the initiatives which Washington has undertaken in the wake of events in Iran and Afghanistan. Furthermore, the shifting currents in U.S. strategy and the developing debate over the first exclusively Reagan defense budget are inextricably bound up with the safeguarding of Western interests in the Middle East. The problems attending any attempt to place credible U.S. military power into the Middle East region are illustrative of the complex global situation confronting the United States.

Moreover, understanding of the historical background underlying American policies toward the Middle East, particularly those applicable to the lands east of Suez, is also essential to comprehension of the evolving U.S. stance in that part of the world. Exploitation of the region's oil resources, the long Arab-Israeli conflict, and the global confrontation between the United States and the USSR have all affected and will continue to influence events in this volatile region.

2.
The Historical Background

PRIOR TO the Second World War, American interests in the Middle East, particularly in and around the Persian Gulf, were confined to the expanding exploitation of oil. Petroleum independent at the time—the United States was the leading exporter—those interests focused on supplying the technological and engineering skills, along with the associated equipment, required to bring these new sources of energy on line. Inherent also was the prospect of vast profits for American international oil companies and the resultant economic benefits flowing to the United States from the accompanying huge favorable balances of trade. It is no exaggeration to assert that, for decades, the American export-import balance sheet was kept in black ink largely due to the return on U.S. investment in Middle East oil exploration and development.

During those years, the British Raj held sway over the nations of the area, by either hegemonistic or colonial means, and the presence of Empire armed forces insured regional political tranquility. No serious external military threat challenged the United Kingdom's domination, and the only bar to unlimited American exploitation of Middle East oil lay in competition generated by oil companies of other advanced industrial nations. Thus, Washington perceived no pressures demanding a regional presence of significant U.S. armed strength—periodic or permanent—to guarantee unfettered operation of the nation's oil companies or to guard against dangers to this country's welfare. Absence of any threat to U.S. national interests was particularly true in North Africa where oil riches still lay hidden beneath its burning sands. Thus, living under the twin umbrellas of domestic energy abundance and a spirit of international isolationism, the United States kept its military forces at home.

This complacent attitude was abruptly shattered with the outbreak of World War II. Isolationism still predominated in the American body politic and severely constrained the more activist nature of President Franklin Delano Roosevelt. Efforts to rebuild the nation's armed forces, which had fallen to dangerously low levels during the 1930s, had to be taken in excruciatingly small steps to avoid not only direct confrontations with the U.S. Congress, but a loud outcry from the American people. Though the war clouds in Europe were visible to Roosevelt long before Hitler's legions actually crossed the Polish frontier, the onset of the war found the United States woefully unprepared to participate in any meaningful way. Moreover, only through careful maneuvering was the American President able to obtain passage of a law, which he interpreted very liberally, providing "lend-lease" support to the embattled West European nations.

The Japanese attack on Pearl Harbor, of course, propelled the United States into the war and galvanized its citizens to prodigious efforts. Long before that happened, however, threats to the Middle East oil fields had materialized. The first to capture the world's attention was Field Marshal Erwin Rommel's drive across North Africa, which came within a whisker of driving the British out of Egypt. Then, following the Nazi invasion of the Soviet Union, German troops stood at the foot of the Caucasus Mountains within reach of Baku and Iran, only a short distance from the major oil fields of the Middle East.

The Allied response was twofold. Great Britain, its traditional dominion over this portion of the globe seriously endangered by the German offensives, fought hard to stave off Rommel's Afrika Corps, eventually turning the German drive back at El Alamein. Once in the war, the United States joined the United Kingdom in opening a military supply line to the hard-pressed Russians through Iran and into the Caucasus. This operation to supply weapons and materiel, desperately needed by the Soviets to stem the Nazi invasion, thus produced the first American military presence in the Middle East.

Troops and equipment from the United States poured into the Persian Gulf region to establish, operate and protect this vital lifeline to the Soviet Union. In North Africa, additional American forces landed in 1942 to join with the British in eventually defeating the Axis powers and ejecting them from the continent. In both instances, therefore, U.S. military commitments to stability and security in the Middle East grew out of American participation in World War II.

With the end of that war, it appeared that the United States would return swiftly to its traditional international posture. Three significant developments, however, were already moving center stage, the consequences of which would drastically alter not only Washington's view of the international scene, but of the role the United States would henceforth have to play thereon. The demise of isolationism was at hand.

First, and most important, the Soviet Union began to demonstrate— even before the fighting came to an end—that it considered the wartime alliance to have been little more than a marriage of convenience. The predatory nature of the Soviet regime manifested itself in the overrunning of all of Eastern Europe and in an obvious reluctance to withdraw from other areas which had been occupied by the Red Army. In the Middle East, this recalcitrance was most clearly evidenced in Iran.

Second, the major nations of Western Europe—Great Britain and France—had nearly exhausted themselves in the long effort to defeat

5

the Axis powers. The United Kingdom, especially, found itself almost destitute economically and hard pressed to maintain the military prowess which had traditionally held its empire together, thereby permitting London to control events in other strategic portions of the globe.

Finally, the British Empire was increasingly beset by the rising tide of nationalism. Everywhere, demands for independence assailed Great Britain, dissidence appearing across the full spectrum from open unrest to armed insurrection. Other colonial powers, particularly France, encountered the same sort of stresses and strains, but the British confronted, by far, the largest problem and were simply in no position to halt the forces marching toward independence.

For a time, London seemed to be making progress in its efforts to limit the damage in prospect for the empire in the wake of India's independence in 1947. During this brief period, the United States moved swiftly to wind down its commitments which had been assumed incident to the war. With the end of the fighting in Europe, American military units left North Africa and their counterparts withdrew from duty stations in the Persian Gulf region. The flow of American military power ran in two directions. Some elements were shifted from Europe to the Far East to take part in the final assault on Japan. The remainder headed for home. With the collapse of Japan, less than four months after Germany's surrender, that flow shifted exclusively toward the continental United States. It seemed apparent that America was about to go back to the same old isolationist posture.

Exploitation of Middle East petroleum resources would, of course, continue. Given British political dominion throughout the region, however, no American military commitment would be required and, therefore, none would be provided. This was particularly true with respect to the area east of Suez. So long as the United Kingdom's domination continued and the British military presence endured, American oil companies would be able to pursue their objectives in relative safety without the U.S. Government bothering to provide any sort of security. In such circumstances, there was obviously no need for Washington to expend resources on military backup for the operation of any international oil company, even though it might be American—whole or in part—and its operations were producing substantial benefits for the United States.

One very important event transpired immediately after the Second World War, however, alerting an already highly suspicious American President—Harry S. Truman—to the changed international circumstances which prevailed in the Middle East. Moscow obdurately refused to pull its troops out of Iran in accordance with the Allied agreement by which they had been inserted in the first place. Here was clear evidence, for the first time, that the communist regime in Moscow espoused the same kind of objectives which had motivated the Tsars. In this instance, it appeared that the Soviet aim was not confined to acquisition of warm-water ports to the south. It also included dominion over the oil resources of the Middle East.

London was appalled at the prospect. The United States, still captive of the euphoric belief that it was and would continue to be energy independent, worried less about the seeming menace to Middle East oil access and more about the implied threat of Soviet expansionism. In the event, the Soviets were forced out of Iran. The apparent pressure which accomplished the task derived from a joint American-British ultimatum. The reality was that the armed forces of both nations had, in the words of Winston Churchill, "melted" away.[1] They had done so to the point that it is extremely unlikely the remaining conventional military strength of the two nations would have given any pause to Premier Joseph Stalin. The determining factor was the then American nuclear monopoly. President Truman's tough words, underscored by the implicit threat of these cataclysmic weapons, did the trick. The Soviets withdrew.

Moscow's obvious intentions—to keep its troops in northern Iran or to establish a Soviet puppet government in Azerbaijan as well as an "independent" Kurdish republic, all clearly aimed at ultimate control of the Iranian oil fields—resurrected historic fears previously generated by the intrigues of the Tsars. It now appeared that leaders of the modern regime in Russia held many of the same views and, further, had expanded their objectives based on growing realization that the advanced industrialized nations of the West were increasingly hostage to the petroleum resources of the Middle East. The gauntlet thus flung down was too obvious to be ignored. To what extent this perception played a role in Truman's calculations is uncertain to this day. The results, however, are manifest. The Soviet Union, having tipped its international hand, was forced to withdraw. Moreover, the evidence, thus presented, suggested to American officials in Washington—for the first time—that the United States had important strategic interests in the region and they would have to be protected. How, to be sure, was another matter.

Along the North African and Middle East littorals of the Mediterranean, an entirely different set of circumstances came into play. As with the region east of Suez, initial American actions after the war centered on returning all military units to the United States. After all, allied hegemony—British and French—had been reestablished, political stability seemed assured, and the United States had no significant national interests at stake in the area. Far to the north, however, events were

---

[1] Winston S. Churchill, *Triumph and Tragedy* (Boston, Mass.: Houghton Mifflin, 1953), p. 573.

building which would make the North African coast an important piece of real estate in U.S. national security planning.

An embryonic Western European Union (WEU), peering eastward, was slowly coming to the conclusion that its member states had just spent six years defeating Nazi Germany only to discover that they now faced an even more implacable foe in the form of the Soviet Union. The United States, with the pre-war spirit of isolationism beginning to reassert itself, initially remained aloof. When the United Kingdom advised Washington that it could no longer carry the burden of Western defense in Greece and Turkey—the Greeks were then beset with a Soviet-backed insurgency—the United States launched the Truman Doctrine and the Marshall Plan, both crafted to shore up Western Europe against the new threat from the USSR. But an incredible Soviet political gaffe changed American attitudes. With imposition of the Soviet-engineered blockade of Berlin in 1948, the fledgling WEU suddenly became the North Atlantic Alliance and acquired a military arm—the North Atlantic Treaty Organization.

In the Mediterranean, the most visible evidence of emerging American activism was the establishment of the U.S. Sixth Task Fleet in 1948.[2] Originally committed to support of the emerging Truman Doctrine and the Marshall Plan, the task fleet quickly assumed larger and more important functions. As its responsibilities grew, this initial force evolved into the famed U.S. Sixth Fleet which has now operated continuously in the Mediterranean Sea for more than three decades.

In light of evolving American commitments to NATO, one of the first concerns of U.S. military planners was the security of the sea lines of communication running through the Mediterranean. Littoral navies—except for that of France—had little to contribute to this task. The Royal Navy, suffering progressive depletion as a result of the severe economic problems facing the United Kingdom—along with the growing demands emanating from a crumbling overseas empire—found itself less and less capable of aiding Alliance security in the Mediterranean.

The United States, therefore, increasingly assumed that burden through the instrument of the Sixth Fleet. Concurrently, it became necessary to establish bases—naval, air and communication—in North Africa not only to support the naval presence in the region but also to be used to stage air attacks—strategic against the Soviet Union, and ground support as well as strategic against those nations constituting the southern flank of Moscow's answer to NATO: the Warsaw Pact. The foremost such installation in the eastern portion of the Mediterranean Basin was the huge

---

[2]M. Cherif Bassiouni, editor, *Issues in the Mediterranean* (Chicago, Ill.: Chicago Council on Foreign Relations, 1975), p. 26.

Wheelus Air Force Base located in Libya. A World War II airfield built and operated by the United States, Wheelus had been deactivated when American forces returned home after the war. In 1948, it was placed back in operation and for the next 20 years was destined to support United States policy not only in defense of NATO but U.S. positions throughout the Middle East as well.

When the Libyan monarch, King Idris, was overthrown in a successful 1969 coup—the 70-year-old ruler was out of the country undergoing medical treatment in Turkey at the time—the new military government, under the direction of an obscure army captain, Muammar al-Qadhafi, immediately demanded and obtained closure of Wheelus along with departure of all American military personnel and their equipment. Today, the United States has no bases in Libya.

East of Suez, President Truman, perceiving a similar need for signals to all concerned, installed a symbol of American international interest. Established on January 1, 1949, the tiny U.S. Middle East Force began operating from facilities leased from Great Britain on the Persian Gulf island of Bahrain. In terms of ships, the force was and always has been minuscule: a flagship and two destroyers, the latter initially borrowed from the Sixth Fleet. The traditional mission of the Middle East Force has been to visit major ports throughout the Indian Ocean region once or twice a quarter, and smaller, more isolated ports at least once a year. The commander of the force extends this coverage by means of an aircraft which permits him to travel to inland capitals and other important cities where he can meet with government and military leaders as well as with U.S. diplomatic representatives.

This tiny naval force has been eminently successful despite its size, since its main mission has always been a politico-military one without the manifest combat role implicit in the makeup, for instance, of the Sixth Fleet. The objective has been to promote goodwill, understanding, mutual respect and acceptance between the American people and those of the countries visited by the ships. Port calls normally encompass general visiting aboard ship by the local inhabitants, athletic contests with local teams, onboard children's parties, as well as luncheons, receptions and formal dinners for host-country government and military leaders. In those ports where charitable assistance is appropriate, Project Handclasp material is distributed to meet local needs. In addition, each ship assembles community assistance teams comprising crew members with a wide variety of useful skills. These teams frequently refurbish hospitals, orphanages or schools, and provide emergency repair or disaster relief assistance when necessary.

The U.S. Middle East Force remained relatively stable in size—flagship and two destroyers—until the 1980 Soviet invasion of Afghanistan. At

9

that time, two additional destroyers were assigned and remain so at present. Periodic deployments of additional American naval forces to the Indian Ocean region, in response to various international crises, will be addressed in detail later.

The essentially steady-state nature of the foregoing American naval presence in the Mediterranean Sea and the Indian Ocean has been maintained across the years despite a remarkable buildup of similar forces in both regions by the Soviet Union.

The Emergence of Global Soviet Sea Power

It has been said that, in recent decades, the Russian Bear has learned to swim. Not only has he done so, but he has accomplished the feat in much of the salt water which covers 75 percent of the planet upon which we live. For a traditionally land-bound and land-oriented nation such as the USSR, this constitutes a development of signal importance.

Subsequent to the Second World War, aggressive designs concocted in Moscow inevitably ran afoul of that salt water whenever Soviet forces arrived at the rimland of the Eurasian land mass. Moreover, as the Bolsheviks had learned during the early days of their revolution, maritime nations—though far removed from a scene of conflict—could nonetheless exploit the seas to bring military power to bear against coastlines around the world.

Most experts date the renaissance in Soviet naval thinking from the late 1950s. Prior to that time, the Red Fleet was deemed to be little more than a means of defending the seaward flanks of the Red Army. The operations of the U.S. Sixth Fleet during numerous crises in the Middle East, however, and other similar demonstrations of Soviet impotence at sea provided an astute Russian naval officer with a golden opportunity to educate the denizens of the Kremlin. That this man—Admiral of the Fleet of the Soviet Union Sergei G. Gorshkov—seized the opportunity is no longer in serious doubt. Moreover, it seems abundantly clear that the humiliating events incident to the Cuban missile crisis of 1962 added further fuel to the sea power fires Gorshkov was then tending inside the walls of the Kremlin.

Appointed to acting command of the Soviet Navy in 1955 by Nikita Khrushchev, and promptly ordered to scrap all major surface warships while concentrating on building "rocket-firing" submarines as well as selling this radical shift in Soviet naval strategy to his naval confreres, Gorshkov set to work. Not only outlasting his powerful benefactor but outmaneuvering him as well, the newly-installed Soviet naval commander proceeded to produce those submarines, but he also constructed a large,

10

modern, sophisticated surface navy. Today, ships of the Soviet fleet are to be found operating in every ocean of the world.

In 1964, for example, the first permanent Soviet naval deployments to the Mediterranean Sea began with entry of the Fifth Eskadra from the Black Sea Fleet.[3] By the mid-1970s, the strength of the Soviet Mediterranean Squadron had risen to an average of 55 ships, including some 12 submarines. This figure contrasts with the roughly 40 warships normally constituting the U.S. Sixth Fleet. During the 1973 Middle East war, Soviet naval strength in the Mediterranean abruptly climbed to an astonishing 96 ships while the famed Sixth Fleet could muster no more than 70. The East-West transformation in those waters could hardly have been more dramatic.

Today, a strikingly similar situation obtains in the Indian Ocean. In 1968, immediately following Great Britain's declaration that all of its military forces would be withdrawn from "East of Suez" by 1971, a Soviet naval squadron entered the Indian Ocean and conducted a four-month tour of the region, including port calls in India, Iran, Iraq, South Yemen, Somalia and Ceylon. The importance Moscow attached to this excursion was highlighted by the fact that the squadron—led by a *Sverdlov*-class heavy cruiser—was met in Bombay and Madras by Gorshkov himself. Close cooperation between the Soviet and Indian navies dates from these two visits. With that cruise, the Red Fleet came to the Indian Ocean to stay. Averaging some 20 ships, the squadron covers the entire region from the Iraqi naval base at Umm Qasr in the north to Port Louis, Mauritius, in the south; from Aden in the west to the Strait of Malacca in the east. Normally, most of its ships are concentrated in the strategic heart of the region: the northwest quadrant. Its steady-state composition has been in marked contrast to that of the much smaller Middle East Force, the latter augmented only at infrequent intervals by ships or task forces from the U.S. Seventh Fleet in the Western Pacific.

---

[3]George Lenczowski, *The Middle East in World Affairs* (Ithaca, New York: Cornell University Press, 1980), p. 705.

3.
The Collapse
of U.S. Middle East Strategy

THE FIRST TERM of President Richard Nixon's Administration (1969-1973) provides a benchmark against which to gauge the Middle East security strategy of the United States. When he took office, the nation ostensibly possessed the military capability to fight, successfully, "2½" wars simultaneously. That is to say, the prime U.S. national security objective was to maintain sufficient armed strength to assist in defending Western Europe against a major Soviet assault, to defeat simultaneously any aggressive move in the Pacific Far East by the People's Republic of China, and at the same time cope with a smaller contingency somewhere else in the world: a revolution in Panama, for instance, which would pose a major threat to the Canal. Together with his National Security Affairs Adviser—Dr. Henry A. Kissinger—the new American President examined existing U.S. armed forces and concluded that the requisite military strength was neither in being, nor in prospect. In short, the "2½" war strategy was little more than a paper exercise which would assuredly be found wanting should it ever be called to account.

Accordingly, a broad analysis of extant U.S. global commitments was initiated, and the so-called Nixon Doctrine was ultimately formulated. Fundamentally, the resultant national strategy held that the United States no longer could or would dedicate itself to unilateral policing of the myriad trouble spots existing around the world. Instead, primary responsibility for maintaining local political stability would have to be assumed by regional countries themselves. Where necessary, the United States would supply the requisite military hardware and training to permit such nations to do the job. If a sufficiently severe external threat materialized—one with which the local countries clearly could not cope—the United States would enter the lists, providing naval and air power as required to make collective resistance effective. In the last resort, American ground forces would be committed to guarantee preservation of regional stability. Specifically, the Nixon Doctrine set forth the following guidelines:[4] (1) Henceforth, the United States would take a more selective approach to its global role—inherited with the termination of the Second World

---

[4]Alvin J. Cottrell and Robert J. Hanks, "The Future Role of Iran," in *The U.S. Role in a Changing World Political Economy: Major Issues for the 96th Congress* (Washington, D.C.: U.S. Government Printing Office, 1979), p. 547.

War—particularly in the wielding of its military power. (2) An increased measure of burden-sharing would have to be assumed by America's allies and friends around the globe insofar as their own defense was concerned. (3) American help (restricted essentially to military equipment and training) would be provided to safeguard the independent posture of regional states and to assist them in maintaining political stability, thereby implicitly helping to safeguard U.S. national interests around the world.

Implementation of this new doctrine was nowhere more evident than in the Persian Gulf. There, it was accompanied by a supplementary approach which, subsequent to 1972, came to be known as the "Twin Pillar" policy. Iran and Saudi Arabia—viewed by Washington as the two most populous and richest nations in the area—would constitute twin stanchions upon which would rest not only the security of the region itself but that of American national interests. Consequently, the U.S. arms locker was thrown open to both countries. In the event, the Shah of Iran spent billions of dollars flowing from his rapidly expanding oil revenues to acquire huge quantities of the latest and most advanced military weaponry produced in the United States. For its part, Saudi Arabia also began to purchase the kinds of modern military equipment which ultimately would allow it to make a meaningful contribution to its own as well as to general Persian Gulf security.

By the mid-1970s, this U.S. doctrine had begun to pay promising dividends. The vacuum created by the 1971 British military withdrawal from East of Suez was beginning to be filled by the local nations of the Gulf. Moreover, the feat was apparently being accomplished well before the Soviet Union could take advantage of the deteriorating strategic situation. Unfortunately, the scheme foundered on the rocks of the Iranian revolution.

With the fall of the Shah of Iran in early 1979, and his ill-fated dynasty's replacement by the chaotic rule of the Ayatollah Ruhollah Khomeini, one of the two pillars precipitately crumbled. Given the military advances which Iran had by then made, there could be little doubt that the revolt marked the collapse of the stronger pillar.

On the opposite side of the Gulf, a credible Saudi Arabian military posture was only beginning to take shape, and it obviously had a very long way yet to go. Thus, the upheaval in Iran marked the breakdown of a heretofore seemingly promising American foreign policy, one originally designed to forestall any Soviet advance into the international power void created in the Persian Gulf and Indian Ocean regions by the 1971 British withdrawal. The Nixon Doctrine, as implemented by the Twin Pillar policy in the Gulf, thus endured for less than a decade. With the overthrow of the Shah, and the virulent anti-Western attitude subsequently manifested by the new Iranian Shiite leadership, Western inter-

13

ests—particularly those of the United States—were suddenly placed in considerable jeopardy.

The foregoing problems were compounded by a growing perception around the world—previously cited—that the prosecution of American foreign and security policies was continuously subject to indecision, vacillation and timidity. Accordingly, credible U.S. fulfillment of bilateral obligations and promises was brought into serious question. Moreover, American allies engaged in multilateral undertakings, such as member states of the North Atlantic Alliance, also began to entertain serious reservations about the viability of the contracts they had signed. If Washington could not be counted upon to meet its international commitments or to protect its own national interests, those who would thereby be forced to shift for themselves faced two options. First, they could turn elsewhere for the military weaponry they required as well as for the primary political and secondary military support to go with it. Or, they could seek some form of accommodation with the international forces which threatened them. In either case, a catastrophic decline in American influence would inevitably ensue. Moreover, should such imperiled nations elect to turn to the Soviet Union or its client states for help, the resultant loss would be suffered by the entire Western bloc.

After the Shah of Iran was toppled and Ayatollah Khomeini seized control, the Carter Administration began to take a serious look at how U.S. Middle East interests might be safeguarded in the future. Initially, the problem was perceived by American national security planners as merely one of containing excesses being exhibited by the fundamentalist Islamic regime Khomeini and his followers seemed determined to establish. Of prime concern in Washington was the prospect that this form of religious virus might be exported to other Arab nations in the region wherein Shiite Moslems were either in a substantial minority or constituted very nearly a majority. The danger that political chaos would eventually spread throughout the Persian Gulf area suddenly became very real. Implications for the uninterrupted flow of oil to the West—in light of the recent Iranian experience—abruptly captured Washington's attention.

Given these possibilities, the outlook for sustained political stability in this critical region of petroleum supply for the industrial West became something less than bright. Then, in response to deteriorating political conditions in Afghanistan, the Soviet Union launched a massive, armed invasion of that mountainous nation, a move which shocked the world community. This manifest extension of the Brezhnev Doctrine—that the world should expect Soviet military force invariably to be used to crush any threat to an established communist regime—to nations not previously members of the immediate post-World War II Soviet bloc, triggered

14

alarm bells all around the globe. More importantly, it propelled a clearly idealistic President of the United States into the real world of power-politics—the one in which we all actually live.

In January of 1980, shaken by the bold exercise of Soviet power in Afghanistan, President Carter stepped up to the rostrum to deliver his annual State of the Union address to the United States Congress and the American people. In that speech, Jimmy Carter confessed that the recent events in Afghanistan had finally awakened him to the reality that the men who ruled in the Kremlin were not reasonable seekers of peace and detente as he had, for the past three years, judged them to be. Newly and belatedly enlightened, using that address as a vehicle, the President drew an American defensive line around the Arabian Peninsula. By so doing, he warned the Soviet Union that further military incursions in that portion of Southwest Asia would inevitably endanger vital U.S. national interests. The implied threat was that should such events materialize, Moscow could expect to find itself confronting American military power, with all the escalatory global and strategic nuclear risks which that would certainly entail. While most Americans applauded this laggardly recognition by the President that their vital interests in the Middle East were once more being placed in serious jeopardy, some of them recalled a somewhat similar speech delivered by U.S. Secretary of State Dean Acheson in early 1950.

Then, too, a U.S. defense line had been sketched. In essence, the earlier one delineated international ramparts which the United States was determined to defend in the event of communist aggression, this time in the Pacific Far East. The trouble with that Acheson speech was the fact that it excluded the Korean Peninsula from the ramparts and, moreover, the Secretary's words failed to make one thing crystal clear: aggression on the peninsula would be deemed by Washington directly to imperil U.S. vital interests. As a result of Acheson's imprecision, the communist regime in Pyongyang mistakenly concluded that the time was ripe to unify Korea under its leadership. Years of bloody warfare then ensued before the North Koreans eventually decided that their goals could not be achieved. One is constrained to speculate that Kim Il Sung and his cohorts never forgave Dean Acheson for so badly misleading them.

With the 1980 Carter speech, those who remembered the traumatic days of the early 1950s wondered if others—particularly the leaders in the Kremlin—would make a similar mistake, this time with respect to opposing aggression on the Iranian side of the Persian Gulf or in Pakistan. Almost immediately after Carter's 1980 pronouncement, his own Secretary of Defense, Harold Brown, let it be publicly known that the United States did not, at the time, possess sufficient deployable military power to enforce the President's warning. The world community was thereby treated to yet another demonstration of the disarray existing within the Carter Administration, a spectacle which further contributed to the already widespread perception of the United States as a "crippled giant." Presumably, Secretary Brown's assessment stemmed from a realistic analysis of the geostrategic truths abounding in the region and the problems associated with any attempts to move relevant U.S. military force to the waters of the Indian Ocean and the Persian Gulf. Furthermore, Harold Brown's analysis must also have come to grips with the complications of putting the troops and equipment ashore, once they arrived on the scene. It can be reasonably inferred that this revelation in Washington commenced with seizure of the American Embassy in Teheran and its staff. The first reaction of the Carter Administration was to order a carrier battle group into the Indian Ocean as a demonstration of concern and determination. Reality, however, promptly entered the picture. Here was a warship whose further production President Carter had consistently vetoed since taking office. With the U.S. Navy reduced to twelve deployable carrier decks, the White House quickly discovered that sustained stationing in the Indian Ocean of just one such ship—together with escorting men-o'-war—would require a commensurate reduction in the aircraft carrier complement of either the Sixth or Seventh Fleets.

When, in response to the subsequent Soviet invasion of Afghanistan, a second American carrier battle group was ordered to join the first one, that reality was reinforced: in order to maintain the two task forces in the Indian Ocean for any extended period, the Sixth and Seventh Fleets would have to be reduced to one aircraft carrier apiece. The net effect of so stretching a severely shrunken U.S. Navy was compounded by similar strains simultaneously inflicted on destroyers and cruisers as well as amphibious elements.

In early November of 1979, when planning got underway to select an appropriate U.S. response to the humiliating hostage situation in Teheran, additional grim realities intruded. The difficulties attending military operations in the desert environment of the Middle East—personnel as well as equipment—immediately came to light. Aside from the fundamental problem of simply transporting U.S. military forces to that distant region in a timely manner, the diminished overall strength of existing American armed forces, coupled with terrain and distance complications within the area, logistic support and myriad other factors, all served to highlight the seemingly intractable dimensions of the problem.

Ignoring the numerous mistakes made from inception through execution of the ill-starred "Blue Light" attempt to rescue the American hostages being held in Teheran, that operation can be used to illustrate many of the complications confronting the United States as it seeks to devise a workable strategy for the Middle East region. When that plan-

16

ning effort began, it quickly became apparent that an almost complete absence of local operating bases available to the United States dictated that any rescue endeavor would have to originate from the sea. Thus, the prime vehicle for mounting such an effort would necessarily be an aircraft carrier. Since the distance to Teheran from the most likely launching site would be on the order of 900 miles, the helicopters—the only feasible means of landing in the center of the city and extracting the hostages—would have to be refueled en route. This meant that tanker aircraft—the Lockheed-built C-130 was chosen—would have to be included in the effort. Given the relatively limited range of that aircraft, it would have to take off from some base near the heart of the Middle East, and en-route fueling would also be required. Moreover, the aircraft would probably be forced to overfly the territory of one or more sovereign countries en route to their ultimate destination.

The flight path followed by the C-130s has never been publicly disclosed. At the time, press reports asserted that the aircraft—carrying fuel, equipment, and the Blue Light rescue team—departed from airbases in Egypt, clearly with the consent of then-President Anwar Sadat, and refueled at the ex-British airbase on the Omani-owned island of Masirah. Those same reports claimed that the operation had not been cleared in advance with the Government of Oman and that Sultan Qaboos had "sent a blistering message" to the U.S. Government about this unauthorized use of his country's air space and territory.[5]

This portion of Blue Light illustrates two aspects of externally mounted military operations being conducted in the Middle East: the need for advance bases from which to stage operations and to sustain them logistically; and the vital issue of overflight and landing rights where air operations are necessary. It must be taken as a certainty that, in an international crisis situation, the diplomatic nicety of requesting and receiving overflight clearances will usually be ignored. A nation with sufficient military power to conduct such operations, despite any resistance presented by an offended country, will surely do so. The Soviet Union, for example, has never shown any reluctance to violate Iranian air space in sending its aircraft into the Indian Ocean, even in times of peace. No rational person could expect Moscow to be less considerate of the precepts of international law in time of war. In view of the Blue Light operation, the same can be said of the United States. This latter factor is significant with respect to any future use of the Rapid Deployment Joint Task Force. With few exceptions, access rights to en-route landing and refueling sites is critical to the success of the RDJTF.

---

[5]William Beecher, "Oman Protests Stopover by U.S.," *Boston Globe*, May 3, 1981, p. 1.

Part of the blame for failure of the rescue mission has been ascribed to "suspended dust clouds" which caused vertigo, disorienting some of the helicopter flight crews, and may well have contributed to those mechanical failures which reduced the number of aircraft below the minimum deemed necessary to complete the rescue. The unique climatic conditions in this part of the world cannot be ignored when contemplating military operations. Special air filters are required, for example, to protect sensitive modern equipment. It is the height of folly to anticipate that combat vehicles designed to fight in Western Europe could be transported to the Middle East and effectively employed in the latter environment. Even at sea, the problem cannot be avoided. Intakes for air-conditioning and electronic equipment must be protected against ingestion of the ever-present sand particles borne aloft by desert winds.

Yet another criticism leveled at the Blue Light effort was the absence of a full-scale rehearsal. Insofar as the RDJTF is concerned, this is a prime consideration. As things currently stand, there is no place around the northwestern Indian Ocean littoral where such a realistic rehearsal of the Force's ability to offload equipment carried by the prepositioned ships and to join those cargoes with incoming airlifted troops can be conducted. Thus, the base situation in the Middle East is clearly a central concern.

In this connection, the 1969 loss of access to Wheelus Air Force Base in Libya has become a major setback in 1982. Even though offset to a considerable extent by Egyptian cooperation, originating with Anwar Sadat's granting of base and overflight rights, the problem cannot yet be deemed solved. Much depends upon the attitude of Hosni Mubarak— and how he will ultimately view American actions in the Arab-Israeli confrontation. So long as those Egyptian bases—airfields in the vicinity of Cairo and the facilities at Ras Banas—remain available to American forces destined for operations in the region "East of Suez," Wheelus will not be missed all that much.

In the northwest quadrant of the Indian Ocean as well as within the Persian Gulf itself the base dilemma is acute. In this connection, the marathon Arab-Israeli conflict exerts decisive influence. It will be recalled that none of the Persian Gulf countries—Saudi Arabia included—greeted the 1980 American requests for base rights with any enthusiasm. Only tiny Bahrain has allowed U.S. naval forces to use its facilities. With this exceedingly constrained exception, no succor is available to American military forces on the Arabian Peninsula side of the Persian Gulf. On the opposite side, of course, there are none at all.

Beyond the Persian Gulf itself, the base problem is only slightly less pressing. With the single exception of the severely limited U.S. facilities constructed at the atoll of Diego Garcia, there has been no location in the Indian Ocean which, in the past, the United States could count on in support of its naval or military forces deployed to that part of the world. Even Diego Garcia is not totally secure. The government of Mauritius recently reiterated its opposition to British control of the atoll and the granting of base rights to the United States. It is not likely that the present British Prime Minister, Margaret Thatcher, will accord serious consideration to these arguments, but the possibility that some succeeding UK government—liberal rather than Tory—would bow to Mauritian sovereignty claims cannot be completely discounted. In short, much of the present American military stance in the Indian Ocean depends on territory controlled by others. This is nowhere more obvious than with respect to the agreements the United States negotiated with various regional countries following the Soviet military invasion of Afghanistan. Somalia, Kenya and Oman—alone among regional states—granted limited "facility" use to the United States.

In this part of the globe, the United States cannot count on access to any full-fledged "base." The political cost of such an arrangement to local governments—abundantly demonstrated by other superpower confrontations—would simply be too high. Insofar as shaikhdoms in the Persian Gulf are concerned, the crux of the matter is traditional American policy toward the Arab-Israeli dispute. So long as Washington is viewed on the global scene as the prime—and sole—international supporter of Israel, no Arab nation except Oman believes it can afford the political costs associated with the granting of U.S. military access to its territory. In this light, it is little wonder that nations within the Persian Gulf turned an exceedingly cold shoulder to the 1979 American requests for base rights.

The foregoing situation has recently been further exacerbated by the Israeli invasion of Lebanon and Tel Aviv's perceived sanctioning of the massacres in Palestinian refugee camps. In both instances, the United States was viewed in most of the Arab world as being the hand maiden of Zionist expansionism.

4.
American Military Forces in the Indian Ocean

A S NOTED, the total American military presence in the Indian Ocean area has historically comprised the three ships and one transport aircraft of the Middle East Force. That pattern was initially broken when an aircraft-carrier group, formed around the nuclear-powered U.S.S. *Enterprise,* entered the Ocean from the Pacific incident to the 1971 Indo-Pakistani War. The next two years saw the American military posture return to its traditionally low level. Then, in 1973, the fourth Arab-Israeli war brought a cycle of Indian Ocean naval augmentations with the appearance of U.S. carrier or cruiser battle groups two to three times a year. Only during these periods did American naval strength in the Indian Ocean either approximate or exceed that routinely maintained there by Moscow.

When the aircraft carrier U.S.S. *Hancock* and her escorting ships entered the Indian Ocean in 1973, the Pentagon announced that the presence was in response to the Soviet naval buildup in the Mediterranean. No one—certainly not the Arab states—swallowed this line. Taking up cruising stations off the southern end of the Arabian Peninsula, the presence of these ships was obviously intended to transmit a stern warning to Arab countries not to oppose U.S. political initiatives then being undertaken by Secretary of State Kissinger. The nature of the signal, however, was never announced publicly.

In late 1979, the United States once again dispatched a powerful carrier task force to the Indian Ocean, this time in response to the seizure of the American Embassy in Teheran, Iran, and the illegal holding, as hostages, of all its employees. The ultimate irony so often overlooked in this instance was that President Jimmy Carter found himself compelled to fall back on assistance from the one warship whose further construction he had consistently vetoed since assuming office: the large-deck carrier. Even so, his travails did not end there.

Less than two months later, the Soviet Union mounted a swift, massive invasion of Afghanistan to prevent the overthrow of the Marxist regime which it had originally sponsored in Kabul. Knowing that there was no credible way the United States could counter this baldly aggressive move, President Carter once again looked around for some kind of response. As before, all he found reasonably available was another carrier group from the U.S. Seventh Fleet in the Western Pacific. Thus, as the 1980s dawned, the United States Seventh Fleet—for more than three decades the main guarantor of Western security in the Pacific Far East—found itself without a single aircraft carrier for the first time since the end of the Second World War.

Subsequently, the United States began to develop plans for a so-called Rapid Deployment Force. In light of regional reactions to the 1973-1980 U.S. initiatives, it is worthwhile to examine the role which any military presence can play in the resolution of international crises, as well as the political pluses and minuses inherent in such use of armed might.

The Military Presence

At the outset, it needs to be said that we all live in a power-political world. Perfect man, as postulated by the famous Swiss-born French philosopher, Jean Jacques Rousseau, obviously does not yet populate this earth. Moreover, he apparently is not yet in sight. Accordingly, one should expect nations to conduct themselves very much as do the less-than-perfect individuals who make up their bodies politic. It necessarily follows that in disputes between sovereign countries, military force is bound to constitute the ultimate arbiter. This does not mean, however, that such force is useful only when all other international avenues have been exhausted and resort to armed prowess offers the sole alternative for settling the matter. Moreover, the threat of military power can often be used to affect negotiations between countries throughout the process of attempting to reach mutually acceptable agreements. It is in this latter context that "presence" plays a useful role short of armed conflict. Designed to signal interest, will and determination, as well as to underline political warnings, military force—properly fashioned, positioned and poised—can frequently deter armed conflict, thereby expediting a negotiated settlement of an international dispute. By the nature of the power it disposes, a *relevant* military force can coerce an adversary or impose caution on his actions, while simultaneously reassuring nearby friends and allies.

Employment of naval forces in this manner is a different and more sophisticated use than the traditionally recognized and frequently maligned "gun-boat diplomacy" which came to be associated with blatant exploitation of colonial and semi-colonial countries, reaching its apogee in Western relations with 18th and 19th century China. Today, the anatomy of the military presence is far better understood than it was in that long-gone era, and its utility extends across a far broader spectrum than in the days of gunboats patrolling the rivers and territorial waters of a disunited and feudal China. The reason for the change is clear. The cataclysmic power of the nuclear weapon has made avoidance of war a prime objective of the world's major nations, and the military presence—whether its power includes a nuclear capability or is confined to conventional weaponry—is most frequently invoked to prevent an incipient crisis from getting out of hand and escalating to the point that the world is threatened with the use of these awesome weapons.

Still, there are times when utilization of a military presence is neither appropriate nor helpful. In some circumstances, for example, its employment merely serves to harden attitudes, thereby rendering achievement of the desired political solution either more difficult or impossible. In the case of the *Hancock*, knowledgeable observers predicted that the battle group's entrance into the Indian Ocean would produce precisely the opposite effect they inferred lay behind its dispatch. That is to say, it most certainly would not intimidate the Arab states; on the contrary, it was more likely to anger them. Nor would it make them any more amenable to those compromises which might further the search for peace. Seen by the Arabs as an attempt to coerce them, it would merely stiffen their resolve not to be pressured into an unfavorable settlement dictated by the traditional benefactor of the Israeli enemy: the United States. Finally, the implied American threat to the oil installations could be expected to provoke counterthreats to blow up the wells and loading terminals as an assured means of keeping them out of alien hands. These and other forecasts proved to be painfully accurate. Here, one must conclude, was an example of the military presence which was not only ill-conceived but did, indeed, produce just the opposite reaction from the one intended.

On the other hand, the appearance of the nuclear-powered aircraft carrier U.S.S. *Enterprise,* with its menacing air group and accompanying escort ships, off the Kenyan coast in 1977 sent a blunt message to Uganda's mercurial leader Idi Amin. In an attempt to exert pressure on the United States, the African dictator had previously rounded up all Americans in the country and then issued a series of thinly veiled threats against their lives. Confronted with the clear capability of the *Enterprise* air group to respond to such action by devastating his entire military establishment along with much of his country, the crafty Amin publicly announced that he had merely called these Americans to his capital for a party at which he planned to thank them for all the services they had rendered to his people.

In other circumstances, the message conveyed by the military presence can be quite different, depending on its use—or misuse. As the Shah of Iran's dynasty crumbled, President Carter exhibited considerable indecision by ordering and then canceling deployment of the carrier U.S.S. *Constellation* from Subic Bay in the Philippines to the Arabian Sea. Among friend and foe alike, this vacillation engendered nagging doubts about the reliability of American commitments to friends and allies as well as fostering perceptions of a serious lack of American will to defend the country's vital interests. These international reactions were destined to play crucial roles when the Soviet Union launched its invasion of Afghanistan, an action which implicitly placed the entire Persian Gulf region in jeopardy.

No one would argue that the presence of any U.S. naval force in the Indian Ocean would have made the slightest difference in the outcome of the Iranian revolution. Nonetheless, the international image of an indecisive, crippled giant, which derived from American inaction, generated considerable adverse impact on the Western political position in this critical region as subsequent events have abundantly demonstrated.

It thus seems clear that, in this power-political world, there *is* a useful place for the so-called military "presence." Astutely planned and executed, such demonstrations of armed prowess can have a beneficial impact in crisis situations. On the other hand, poorly planned uses of such a presence or their improper application can spawn international complications of major dimensions. This was most assuredly true of the *Hancock* cruise in late 1973 and, a year later, of the U.S. carrier *Constellation's* excursion into the Persian Gulf itself. In the latter instance, unfortunately, it appeared that lessons derivable from the mistake made in 1973 had not been absorbed in Washington.

5.
The Bases Problem:
Diego Garcia and Elsewhere

EARLY IN THE 1960s, military planners in Washington began to worry about the American capability to project power into the Indian Ocean region. It seemed obvious to them that the rumored forthcoming British military withdrawal from "East of Suez" would leave a huge political vacuum. Moreover, they were concerned that the Soviet Union would move with alacrity to fill that void.[6] Subsequent developments testified to the accuracy of their foresight. More than a decade later U.S. national interests included not just concern over Moscow's expansionism, but the fear that Soviet movement into the Persian Gulf and Indian Ocean would pose threats to a critical strategic material: petroleum.

By that time, maintenance of regional political stability, no longer a responsibility accepted by London or the British military, was central to the continued flow of oil to the West in general and to America in particular. If the United States were to play a meaningful political role in the region, Washington would clearly have to possess the military capability to back up its diplomatic and economic initiatives. Such considerations brought into focus the acute problem of access to military bases and facilities which had increasingly haunted responsible American officials. Their concerns corroborated the strategic assessments of those planners who, in the early 1960s, had taken the first steps to solve the specific issue of U.S. bases in the Indian Ocean.

At the end of the Second World War, the American military enjoyed more or less free access to some 150 military bases and facilities around the world. In effect multiplying the power of the nation's armed forces, they permitted the United States to discharge its global commitments while maintaining far fewer active forces than otherwise would have been required. Since that war, however, the number of those bases and facilities has undergone a steady decline. Eroded by the flooding tide of nationalism, fiscal retrenchment on the part of the United States, and abrupt shifts in the international political climate, the total had dropped to around 30 by the early 1970s.

---

[6]Elmo R. Zumwalt, Jr., and Worth H. Bagley, "West Posed to Retain Island Base," *Journal of Commerce,* July 24, 1980, p. 4.

Diego Garcia

In the Indian Ocean region, the United States had only the tiny and tenuous naval foothold on Bahrain. Almost all of the bases previously owned or controlled by the colonial powers were gone, and the few positions the United States had established during the war had been liquidated as well. As U.S. strategists perceived the problem, it was acute. Protecting American interests in this remote body of water and its adjacent littoral nations, situated some 12,000 nautical miles from American shores, posed major problems of stationing and then maintaining there a military force of significant size and capability. The search for a usable base, above all one politically secure, was therefore begun. Initial attention centered on island territories still belonging to Great Britain.

In the western reaches of the Indian Ocean, searchers thought they had found one in the British-owned Aldabra Islands, lying some 200 miles northwest of the northern tip of Madagascar. Fairly distant from the entrance to the Persian Gulf—one distinct disadvantage—it nevertheless was much nearer than any other available base with the single exception of the limited mooring and reprovisioning facilities at Bahrain. This projected solution, however, never got off the ground.

Formerly a part of the Seychelles, Aldabra was detached in 1965 to become an element in the new British Indian Ocean Territory (BIOT). London established the BIOT because of the islands' potential for meeting future armed force requirements. British military commanders believed they would be needed—given the progressive loss of former colonies throughout the region as the postwar nationalist movement accelerated—to provide operating bases from which to safeguard military and trade routes between the United Kingdom and Australia, as well as with the rest of the Pacific Far East. Accordingly, London planned in 1967 to build an air staging facility on Aldabra. There was ample room on the atoll for a 12,000-foot runway. Moreover, it boasted an anchorage in the main channel leading to the lagoon. But the plan came immediately under attack from conservation groups dedicated to preserving the island's unique wildlife. Aldabra is a rare example of a coral atoll with an ecosystem largely untouched by man: nearly 10 percent of its animal, plant and insect species can be found nowhere else on earth. In a sense, it can be considered the Galapagos Islands of the Indian Ocean. Faced with cuts in defense spending as well as the environmentalists' protests—which quickly grew to international proportions—the British Government abandoned the project and ultimately returned the Aldabra Islands to the Seychelles when the latter achieved independence in 1976.

With this option closed, U.S. attention shifted to the atoll of Diego Garcia in the Chagos Archipelago. Also a part of the BIOT, this coral

25

outcropping is claimed by Mauritius, although there is some argument about the validity of the assertion. At the time of this archipelago's incorporation into the BIOT, Diego Garcia's 500 contract copra workers—then the only inhabitants—were resettled in the Seychelles and Mauritius by the British Government. Today there are no indigenous population difficulties. The Ramgoolam Government of Mauritius and its leftist successor, reportedly encouraged by Moscow, have called for return of the chain. It is not likely, however, that London will accord these demands serious consideration.

The most important strategic drawback of Diego Garcia centers on the fact that the atoll lies some 2,500 sea miles from the entrance to the most critical portion of the Indian Ocean: the Strait of Hormuz, which constitutes the sole maritime access to the Persian Gulf and the gargantuan reserves of crude petroleum lying about its periphery. For nations conditioned to exploiting the seas freely and using them not only to insure their well-being but to fend off the efforts of those who would deny such use, this distance is crucial. To the sailor, accustomed to steaming at the most economical speed his warship can make—about 15 knots—that means a seven-day voyage from Diego Garcia to the Strait of Hormuz. Even at a more urgent 25-knot speed of advance, the trip would take more than four days just to reach the Strait. It requires little imagination to envisage what could transpire in the Persian Gulf region during such a critical four- or seven-day period. Thus, while an American naval presence in the Indian Ocean—supported from Diego Garcia—enhances, by an order of magnitude, U.S. ability to respond to threats posed to the continuous flow of Middle East oil and to aid American friends and allies in the region, maritime power based on the atoll could well arrive too late.

To be sure, one would not expect a U.S. Navy aircraft carrier battle group to be spending its time swinging to anchors at Diego Garcia while an incipient crisis began to brew in the Persian Gulf area. Most assuredly, that group would be at sea, steaming within easy striking distance of any extraregional forces which might be poised to endanger either the flow of oil or the future viability of a friendly regime within the Gulf. In such circumstances, Diego Garcia would serve primarily as a logistics base through which the wherewithal to keep that carrier battle group on station would be funneled. Since, absent such a facility located in the central Indian Ocean, essential support—men, fuel, food, repair parts—would have to come from Subic Bay in the distant Philippines or from even further removed depots on the East Coast of the United States, the value of Diego Garcia is abundantly evident.

Even so, elements within the United States Congress have consistently objected to development of the limited facilities originally envisioned for this remote base. Former Senator John Culver (Democrat, Iowa), for instance, steadfastly opposed the expenditure of any funds for the base and pressured the President to undertake negotiations with the Soviet Union aimed at "demilitarization" of the entire Indian Ocean. It is difficult to reconcile the posture of Senator Culver and others of like views with the obvious international threats to U.S. national interests which abound in the region today. This is especially so in light of recent Soviet actions in Afghanistan.

Insofar as the United States is concerned, the importance of Diego Garcia clearly lies in its geostrategic position—distance from the Persian Gulf notwithstanding—as well as its uniqueness as the only politically secure base in the entire region. From this heretofore barren atoll it is now possible to operate combatant naval and air forces in a manner which fills the power vacuum created by the 1971 British military withdrawal, to support and protect forward deployed forces, and to station the newly-devised Rapid Deployment Force (RDF) ships, prepositioned with heavy combat equipment which can be joined with lightly-armed U.S. troops airlifted to the region. In addition, the island can accommodate the logistics aircraft and ships required to reinforce and supply U.S. and allied forces assigned to the Indian Ocean. Even given the considerable distance lying between Diego Garcia and the Strait of Hormuz, the foregoing potential of the atoll is impressive.

Recognizing Diego Garcia's importance, the American Government— in the wake of the Iranian Revolution and the Soviet invasion of Afghanistan, and over objections of those in the U.S. Congress who still failed to perceive the developing economic and political realities in the Indian Ocean—finally took the decision to expand Diego Garcia's capabilities.

The atoll itself—lying below the equator at approximately the same latitude as Dar es Salaam, Tanzania, and Jakarta, Indonesia, and almost equidistant between them, and a little less than 1,000 miles south of the tip of India—is small in size. The sand-covered top of the coral reef extends about 36 miles in a rough U-shape, the open end pointing to the northwest. In spite of this extent, the atoll is narrow in most places along most of its convoluted length and thus encompasses only 10 square miles of usable land. In 1966, the United States negotiated a 50-year lease with the United Kingdom for base rights on the atoll. Five years later, U.S. Navy Seabee teams began construction of an airfield and a communications station.[7]

Over the span of the next decade and a half, Diego Garcia's fortunes oscillated sharply, mostly as a result of strong opposition periodically

---

[7]"Digging in at Diego Garcia," *Time*, July 14, 1980, p. 29.

brought to bear by a small minority in the U.S. Congress that refused to accept the growing strategic importance of the Indian Ocean in United States security calculations. When Jimmy Carter became President of the United States in 1977, he held similar views.

At the very outset of his Administration, he sent his Secretary of State, Cyrus R. Vance, to Moscow with a radical plan to reduce the numbers of American and Soviet strategic nuclear weapons. Leonid Brezhnev listened to the proposal and then, figuratively, threw the American Secretary out on his ear. To salvage at least something from that naive and abortive international initiative, President Carter directed Vance to offer Brezhnev three other subjects for negotiation. One of them concerned the presence of U.S. and Soviet military power in the Indian Ocean.

In March of 1977, following White House instructions, Secretary Vance suggested to the Kremlin leadership that the United States and the Soviet Union begin negotiations aimed at "demilitarization" of the entire Indian Ocean area. The belief that such an outcome would benefit the United States and the West was most certainly one of the more misguided forays into the foreign affairs arena engineered by the new American President. It was immediately and abundantly clear to many strategists in the nation that the notion was not only seriously flawed, but that such negotiations were manifestly fraught with danger.[8]

Fortunately for the West, subsequent Soviet machinations in and around the Horn of Africa generated second thoughts in the minds of those in control of the new American Administration. Washington ultimately placed the Indian Ocean initiative on the back burner. It was not, however, abandoned. Ensuing developments in Iran and Afghanistan have made it highly unlikely that negotiations will be resurrected in the foreseeable future. Nonetheless, they had progressed far enough before being put aside to guarantee that the embryonic base at Diego Garcia would have been one of the first casualties on the American side.

Construction at Diego Garcia has subsequently proceeded and, in recent months, accelerated. Today, the airstrip is being lengthened and hardstand parking areas provided to accommodate the largest combat aircraft in the U.S. inventory. The communications station is in full operation and an L-shaped pier has been built, extending from the beach into the deeper waters of the lagoon. With the dredging of its lagoon and entrance channel, and construction of various storage facilities, particularly for fuel, Diego Garcia is beginning to achieve the capabilities of some of the advanced bases fashioned by the United States in the Pacific during World War II.

---

[8]See Robert J. Hanks, "The Indian Ocean Negotiations: Rocks and Shoals," *Strategic Review*, Winter 1978, for a detailed analysis.

Other Facilities in the Indian Ocean

Shaken by events in Iran and worried about Soviet designs on the Persian Gulf, the Carter Administration also looked elsewhere in the Indian Ocean for support facilities. Diego Garcia—so far removed from the Gulf—did not by itself seem adequate. Ports with adjacent commercial airfields—much nearer to the strategic focal point, the Strait of Hormuz—were clearly needed. If such facilities could be acquired, logistic support could be flown in, transported to the port area, and then loaded aboard waiting warships for onward movement to the fleet at sea. Personnel, mail, and priority materials of relatively small bulk could be ferried directly to the battle groups by twin-engined Carrier Onboard Delivery (COD) aircraft. Moreover, if these same ports could be used as logistics storage areas, the difficulties inherent in maintaining combat forces at the extreme end of a long supply pipeline would be further alleviated. The imperatives associated with military deployments to the Indian Ocean thus compelled the American Administration to sound out regional attitudes with respect to providing such assistance.

After the Iranian Revolution, a U.S. negotiating team was dispatched to the Middle East area to explore the possibilities. In countries around the Persian Gulf, the team met with something less than an enthusiastic reception and found little evidence that any of them were disposed to cooperate. Outside the Gulf, however, the response was markedly different. In Oman, where Sultan Qaboos is understandably worried about possible renewal of the Marxist-inspired rebellion in the western province of Dhofar, it appeared that agreement might well be reached on the use of port and airfield facilities near Muscat along with the former British military airfield located on the offshore island of Masirah. Kenya, an East African nation which had long welcomed warships wearing the Stars and Stripes to its harbor at Mombasa, was expected to react in a similarly encouraging manner. Finally, as a result of Soviet maneuvering in Ethiopia after the overthrow of Emperor Haile Selassie and seizure of power by Lieutenant Colonel Mengistu Haile Mariam's Marxist-oriented military junta, it seemed possible that President Mohammed Siad Barre of Somalia might greet American overtures with some degree of enthusiasm. With these possibilities identified, the campaign to obtain additional facilities to support an increased American presence in the Indian Ocean region began in earnest.

Then, in late December 1979, the region was treated to a spectacle which sent tremors racing through its various capitals and added urgency to the American search for ways of establishing a meaningful military capability in the area: armed forces of the USSR invaded Afghanistan. At once, this brutal action shocked many of the regional states out of

29

their euphoric complacency and galvanized the United States Government to take further action to protect its vital interests in the region. One of the first American moves was to speed up the ongoing negotiations for additional military support facilities around the Indian Ocean littoral.

Initial success came in Oman.[9] In early June 1980, agreement was reached whereby the United States would be permitted to use the ports of Matrah (Mina Qaboos) and Salalah (Mina Raysut) along with airfields at Seeb, Thumrait, and on the island of Masirah, the latter boasting an austere military air base originally built and operated by Great Britain. Under the agreement with Oman, the United States would be permitted to stock some limited amounts of logistic supplies ashore, transport high priority supplies by air through Omani airfields as well as through the ports by ship, and use the airfields for emergency landings by carrier aircraft. Essentially covering the approaches to the Strait of Hormuz, these facilities would thus greatly ease the problems of keeping one or more naval battle groups on station in the Arabian Sea and Gulf of Oman where they are within easy striking distance of the Persian Gulf itself.

On June 26, another set of diplomatic notes was signed in Nairobi whereby Kenya granted the same sort of access to American military units.[10] Here, the port of Mombasa, its adjacent Embakasi airport, and a second airfield located at Nanyuki about 90 miles north of Nairobi, were involved. All have been used in the past by the U.S. Navy, but the new agreement permitted increased access by ships and aircraft as well as storage of some logistics support ashore.

Finally, in mid-August, Somalia and the United States initialed an agreement covering similar American use of airfields and port facilities at Mogadishu and Berbera.[11] The latter, originally developed into an advance naval base by the Soviet Union, places American naval and air forces in close proximity to the vital Bab el Mandeb, the southern gateway to the Red Sea, as well as directly across from Soviet base facilities situated in Aden and along the South Yemeni coastline, including the island of Socotra.

In each of the foregoing cases, the United States has agreed to provide varying amounts of economic and military aid to the countries involved in exchange for access to the facilities, as well as to fund extensive modernization of some of those installations. No "bases" in the normal sense of the word will be established. Given the political sensitivities in each of the countries, and to minimize Soviet opportunities to play to radical

---

[9]"U.S., Kenya in Accord on Allowing Greater Use of Port Facilities," *Washington Star*, June 28, 1980, p. 12.
[10]*Ibid.*
[11]"Somalia Agrees to Let U.S. Use Ports, Airstrips," *Washington Post*, August 21, 1980, p. Al.

elements within them, the U.S. military presence ashore will be maintained at austere levels and project an appropriately low profile.

The largest controversy attended the negotiations with Somalia. A nation which no outside power has ever been fully able to control, Somalia is currently at loggerheads with Ethiopia over possession of the Ogaden region. Populated by nomadic tribes which roam to and fro across an ill-defined, colonially-drawn frontier they can neither see nor comprehend, the Ogaden has been a long-standing bone of contention between these two East African nations. With Soviet and Cuban troops in Ethiopia actively backing the Marxist regime in Addis Ababa, some officials in the United States fear that a U.S.-Somali agreement could pose the danger that the United States would be drawn into this internecine dispute.[12] Specifically, these people are concerned that the unpredictable Somalis, assurances to the contrary notwithstanding, will continue their efforts to take the Ogaden by force of arms. Whether they employ American-supplied arms or not, there is a perceived peril that the United States could be drawn in while safeguarding the installations at Berbera, for example, and find themselves directly confronting Ethiopian or Cuban troops.

The foregoing danger aside, it is clear that the Carter initiative has borne considerable fruit, and the United States appears to have engineered access to a network of facilities in the northwest quadrant of the Indian Ocean to support the increased military presence which seems destined to acquire at least semi-permanent status. With respect to U.S. commitments in the Persian Gulf area, the bases problem has caused difficulties west of Suez as well.

The Base Problem West of Suez

The rise to power of Colonel Qadhafi significantly complicated American planning for the region west of Suez. Loss of the Wheelus airbase hurt badly. Given the reluctance of NATO nations to become collectively involved at all in contingencies beyond the Alliance's formal boundaries, the United States has been forced to face up to an unpleasant reality. Experience with the 1973 airlift to Israel, and the more recent flight of an Air Force squadron of F-15 fighters to Saudi Arabia after the fall of the Shah of Iran, demonstrated that bases in Western Europe and the Mediterranean could not be counted upon in any Middle East crisis. More reliable alternatives had to be found. In no circumstance is this more important than with respect to airlifting sizable numbers of U.S.

---

[12]"U.S. Concludes Deal to Use Somali Base," *Washington Star*, August 22, 1980, p. 1.

troops to some hot spot in the Persian Gulf region. Prepositioning of heavy equipment and supplies can be handled by sealift without requiring the consent of any other nation. Overflight and refueling rights, however, are quite another matter.

Thus, strategic planners in Washington began to look for base-right possibilities in the Eastern Mediterranean. Here, a fallout from the Camp David agreements manifested itself when Anwar Sadat offered to grant the United States use of the Egyptian base at Ras Banas on the Red Sea coast. Unconfirmed reports at the time held that the U.S. C-130 transports, which supported the ill-starred attempt to rescue the American hostages being held at the U.S. Embassy in Teheran, had been staged through Ras Banas. There is little doubt that use of the facilities on this spur of land jutting into the Red Sea would add considerably to American ability to put ground and air combat units into the Persian Gulf region quickly.

Press reports in early August 1980 that agreement had been reached on the use of Ras Banas were denied by the State Department. Subsequent queries elicited the statement that this was a "technical" denial inasmuch as the deal had not yet been "signed, sealed and delivered." Nonetheless, it is known that President Sadat had given his full blessing to the project, and the Department of Defense Budget which went to the Congress in January 1981 contained funds for implementing the agreement.[13] It thus seems clear that the United States was well on the way to making up for the loss of Wheelus.

In a second initiative, undertaken in June of 1980, 12 U.S. F-4E Phantom jet fighters landed at Cairo West Airbase after a 13-hour flight from Moody Air Force Base in Georgia. The aircraft arrived at the invitation of Anwar Sadat to conduct three months of training exercises with their Egyptian counterparts.[14] They joined a sister squadron of 35 Phantoms which had earlier been sold to Egypt by the U.S. Government. Billed as a joint training exercise, it appeared to serve two American objectives. First, of course, was the requirement to gain experience flying and operating in the unique environment of Middle East deserts. Second, U.S. pilots and maintenance crews would provide invaluable training to the Egyptians in handling the complex Phantom jets.

In Egypt, as elsewhere, the United States will invest heavily in exchange for use of the forward facilities. At Ras Banas, for example, it is estimated that the ultimate price tag for modernizing the airfield and installing those admittedly austere facilities designed to accommodate, temporarily, a full division of U.S. Army troops and their support personnel will

---

[13]"Egypt Base Could Cost $400 Million," *Washington Post*, August 26, 1980, p. A1.
[14]"Vital Partner: Building the Cairo Connection," *Time*, July 28, 1980, p. 44.

approach $400 million. Unconfirmed reports in late August 1980 held that Egypt had also agreed to American use of the harbor at Ras Banas as a contingent naval base. This is to say, should a Moslem nation be threatened and U.S. naval use of Ras Banas be required, it would be made available. Even such contingency use, however, would probably require some degree of modernization, and the foregoing U.S. price tag at Ras Banas would go up accordingly. The American ability to move significant military power to the Persian Gulf region is thus undergoing dramatic improvement, and the prospects for further gains are clearly on the horizon.

6.
The Current U.S. Military Posture in the Middle East

The Eastern Mediterranean

IN THE Eastern Mediterranean, the most striking feature of the U.S. military presence is the Sixth Fleet. On station now for more than three decades, this aggregation of warships has come to symbolize American commitment to the defense of NATO Europe. Over the years, of course, the missions of this formidable naval force have gradually evolved and are considerably different now than in the early days of the Sixth Task Fleet.

Perhaps the most profound shift has been elimination of its strategic nuclear responsibilities. In the opening years of the 1950s, carrier aircraft from the Sixth Fleet were assigned targets in the nation's overall nuclear strike plan aimed at the Soviet Union. With the advent of sea-launched ballistic missiles, however, those missions were transferred to U.S. Polaris submarines with carrier aircraft gradually reverting to primary concentration on tactical attack missions, conventional and nuclear.

Today, a primary mission of the Sixth Fleet is to conduct tactical strikes in support of NATO ground operations directed at the Warsaw Pact's southern flank. They could be either nuclear or conventional, depending on the course of the war. Elimination of Pact sea power from the Mediterranean and safeguarding the sea lines of communication through the length of that sea are also prime tasks for the Sixth Fleet. All of the foregoing missions, of course, are designed to defend NATO against the threat posed by the Soviet Union and its East European allies.

Of hardly less importance to the United States is the part which the Sixth Fleet is capable of playing in furthering U.S. national interests throughout North Africa and the Mediterranean portion of the Middle East. On numerous occasions in past years the Fleet has performed precisely this function, the most recent example being a face-off with the Soviet Mediterranean squadron during the fourth Arab-Israeli war. In this instance, the remarkable rise of the Soviet Navy was clearly evidenced when Moscow was able to increase its naval strength in the Mediterranean to more than 90 ships while the Sixth Fleet could boast only 70. Previous to that confrontation, the Sixth Fleet figured prominently in backing up President Eisenhower's ultimatum to the United Kingdom, France and Israel during the 1956 Middle East war when the former two nations attempted to seize the Suez Canal and Israel grabbed the Sinai Peninsula.

Again, during the Lebanon crisis of 1958 and the Jordanian crisis of 1970, movement of the main striking power of the Sixth Fleet—carrier aircraft and amphibious forces—to the waters of the Eastern Mediterranean served, in large measure, to prevent events from getting out of hand.

Today, the U.S. Sixth Fleet averages about 40 warships, as it has over the past years. Its main capability to project power is concentrated in its two aircraft carrier battle groups. The fighter and attack aircraft aboard these ships can range far inland and represent a major capacity to inflict punishing damage on an enemy. The Marine amphibious contingent, which forms a part of the Sixth Fleet, has demonstrated its unique abilities on several occasions, most notably with the landing in Lebanon in 1958, well ahead of the U.S. air and ground units which eventually arrived from Western Europe, and more recently in support of efforts to establish peace in Lebanon in 1982. The importance of the Marine amphibious group stems from the fact that it can respond swiftly—the timeliness of its insertion often preventing an incipient crisis from escalating into full-scale warfare. In essence, the U.S. Marines constitute a fire brigade designed to extinguish a small blaze before it can become an international conflagration.

As for the remaining elements of American military prowess, the Army and Air Force, their permanently deployed strength in the Eastern Mediterranean is concentrated exclusively in Southern Europe. While in the past they have been able to move to hot spots in the Middle East (Lebanon in 1958, for example), that kind of flexibility seemed to come to an end with the 1973 Middle East war. At that time, NATO nations—with the sole exception of Portugal—made it abundantly clear that they did not want their territory used in any way for operations outside the NATO defensive area. Especially, they did not want to expose themselves to Arab charges that military bases within their borders were being used by the United States to conduct operations—resupply of Israel, for instance—which might harm Arab interests. Thus, it is highly unlikely that the American armed forces currently stationed on the West European continent will, in the future, have complete freedom to deploy to the Middle East in crisis circumstances—unless their mission is to protect one or more Arab states from a threat mounted by the Soviet Union.

An exception to the foregoing assessment rests in the U.S. Air Force deployments to Egypt which have taken place in recent years. During the height of the Iranian crisis, for example, Washington dispatched airborne, early-warning aircraft (AWACS) to the Middle East to demonstrate American interest in the security of Egypt and Saudi Arabia. There, they flew from the Egyptian airfield at Qena situated on the Nile, some 300 miles south of Cairo. And in mid-1980, as previously noted, a squadron of American F-4 fighters, operating out of Cairo West, conducted joint training exercises with the Egyptian Air Force. Finally, when the Iran-Iraq war threatened to spill over into other countries of the Persian Gulf, the United States again sent a contingent of AWACS aircraft, this time to bases in Saudi Arabia. In this instance, the objective was to augment the Kingdom's air defense capability should Iran attempt to make good on its threat to strike nations "supporting" Iraq. Thus, despite the 1968 ejection of U.S. Air Force personnel from Wheelus in Libya, the United States Navy is no longer always alone along the northern shores of the Eastern Mediterranean. At the moment, however, this is the extent of American military deployments to the Mediterranean end of the Middle East. On the opposite side of the Suez Canal, the situation has undergone dramatic changes in the past year or so, and further changes are in prospect.

East of Suez

In the Indian Ocean-Persian Gulf region, the U.S. military presence has been relatively stable for some three decades. As previously indicated, American troops stationed in the area during World War II were all withdrawn following termination of hostilities in Europe. From then until 1949, the Persian Gulf was deemed a strategic backwater by the United States and suffered neglect as thorough as any other single portion of the globe. Under the pressure of emerging Soviet expansionism, however—most blatantly exhibited by Moscow's obvious determination to retain military forces in Iran—President Truman elected to place a small naval presence in the region. Thus, the three-ship U.S. Middle East Force came into being, homeported on the island of Bahrain. Using facilities at the end of the Jufair Peninsula leased from the British, who then still exercised control of foreign and defense matters for the shaikhdoms in the Gulf, this U.S. naval contingent initiated a pattern of cruises and port visits throughout the Indian Ocean. More political than military—given its comparative combat impotence—the Force was designed to demonstrate American interest in a low-key manner while serving as a signal to the Soviet Union that the United States would not tolerate political or military incursions by unfriendly external powers.

Although the military capabilities of the Middle East Force were then and traditionally have been minuscule, the American flags flying from these ships conveyed an implicit warning. Should a crisis erupt, one which Washington believed might imperil American interests, far more powerful U.S. naval forces could quickly arrive in the Indian Ocean, either from the Sixth Fleet in the Mediterranean, from the U.S. Seventh Fleet in the Pacific Far East, or from both. This is precisely what happened during the Indo-Pakistani War in 1971, incident to the fourth Arab-Israeli war in 1973, and again following the fall of the Shah of Iran. In the latter instance, subsequent to the Soviet invasion of Afghanistan and conforming to the previous pattern, Washington ordered a second aircraft carrier battle group into the Indian Ocean as one of the several moves President Carter belatedly made to shore up American military capabilities.

When the U.S. Administration decided to augment American naval forces in the Indian Ocean on a long-term basis, however, President Carter suddenly found himself confronting a hard reality he had done a good deal to create. Between 1968 and 1979, the overall strength of the United States Navy had been allowed to decline from over 900 men-o'-war to fewer than 450. It was immediately and painfully obvious that ships for these new responsibilities in the Indian Ocean could only be assembled at the expense of extant international U.S. commitments elsewhere, primarily those in the Western Pacific and the Mediterranean Sea.

For the long term, however, a better alternative had to be devised. In the event, a decision was taken in Washington to reduce to one the historic two-carrier presence in the Mediterranean as the only feasible means of meeting the new challenges in Southwest Asia. Thus, when it came time to relieve the first Seventh Fleet carrier group, the nuclear-powered U.S.S. *Nimitz,* accompanied by two similarly powered escort ships—*California* and *Texas*—were detached from the Sixth Fleet in the Mediterranean and sailed at 25 knots for the Indian Ocean via the Cape of Good Hope.

This high-speed voyage—made without the necessity for pausing at sea or stopping at various ports en route to refuel—clearly demonstrated the unique advantages of nuclear power in modern warship construction. Further, the American press reported in mid-1980 that, by fall, 42 dredges would complete widening and deepening the Suez Canal sufficiently to permit U.S. aircraft carriers to sail between the Mediterranean Sea and the Indian Ocean.[15] Such transits have now been made, and the resultant reduction in transit time—as compared with that required by the route around the Cape of Good Hope—has appreciably eased the U.S. Navy's problems in meeting commitments in both regions.

Beginning in 1980, two aircraft carrier battle groups were maintained in the Indian Ocean with traditional carrier assignments to the Sixth and Seventh Fleets reduced by half. Even then, it was apparent that such a pace could not be indefinitely sustained. Vice Admiral Staser M. Hol-

---

[15]"Widening the Suez for Flattops," *Newsweek,* July 7, 1980, p. 15.

comb, then Director of Program Planning for the Navy Department, made this abundantly clear:

Right now we have an average of 4¾ carriers deployed, and that's a little more than the system will bear. When you do that on a prolonged basis, you grind yourself down to a halt. Something's got to give here in the course of the next year. We cannot keep two carriers deployed in the Indian Ocean, one in the Mediterranean and one in the Western Pacific with an extra one in one of those places most of the time, the way we've been doing. We can't keep it up indefinitely.[16]

The same case may be made with respect to the Marine amphibious groups stationed at overseas locations. As an additional part of the U.S. buildup in the Indian Ocean, a five-ship, 1800-man Marine amphibious group was originally sent from the Seventh Fleet. When it came time to relieve this force, its replacement had to be drawn from the Mediterranean. Again, the strains of trying to meet—as the U.S. Chief of Naval Operations, Thomas B. Hayward, had put it—"a three-ocean requirement with a one-and-a-half ocean navy,"[17] were beginning to tell. In the latter instance, Admiral Holcomb's carrier group assessment was equally valid.

The U.S. Navy took one other action in 1979, this one directed at the Middle East Force. At the same time the first carrier group was dispatched for duty in the Indian Ocean, two destroyers were added to the Middle East Force, raising its permanent strength to five ships. Other than the short period in 1974 when a Military Sea Transportation Service (MSTS) oiler was assigned in response to the Arab oil embargo, this is the only instance in three decades when the tiny naval force totaled more than three ships.

---

[16]Ann Hughey, "The Age of Aircraft Carrier Diplomacy," *Forbes*, July 21, 1980, p. 57.
[17]*Ibid.*

7.
Personnel Problems and Military Readiness

ONE CANNOT evaluate the American military presence in the Middle East without addressing the problem of personnel. In recent years, under the pressure of heavy inflation, along with Administration decisions to bar offsetting increases in military pay—exemplified by the so-called pay cap—all the American armed services have encountered severe difficulties in recruiting, as well as in retaining, adequate numbers of personnel. In this regard, the U.S. Navy has been particularly hard hit, especially in the middle-level enlisted ratings where most of the technical operation and maintenance skills are to be found. Overall shortages of personnel, enlisted as well as officer, have resulted primarily from the attempt in the 1970s to staff the armed forces on a completely volunteer basis. Until late 1981, the Services were consistently unable to attract recruits and retain trained manpower in sufficient quantity and of adequate quality.

The situation was sufficiently bad at the entry level, but it was far more debilitating in the higher enlisted ratings where skilled technicians were leaving the services in droves. The latter condition was described to the Congress as a virtual "hemorrhage" of trained personnel. In the latter part of 1981 and early 1982, that exodus slowed appreciably. As a result, the chiefs of the various armed services were able to tell Congressional committees that the personnel crisis was definitely abating.

Unfortunately, two factors, giving little comfort to those who viewed the problem in the long term, were operative. First, of course, was the growing recession in the United States. Those old enough to remember were acutely aware that during the great depression of the 1930s, the United States Navy found itself besieged with enlistment applications from college graduates. No other opportunities were available. A similar situation existed in early 1982. Second, a sizable pay increase legislated in 1980 offset, to some extent, previous years of "pay capping." If either of these factors changed—particularly an upward turn in the nation's economy—the aforementioned rosy picture would assuredly turn black once again. And, as before, the resultant personnel shortages would likely produce yet another "hemorrhage" of skilled personnel from the Navy. Moreover, the loss of skilled, middle-level enlisted personnel which had occurred in the preceding decade will take years to offset.

While all of the foregoing personnel difficulties are severe, and some long-term solution to the conditions creating them must be found, it should be understood that the United States Navy nevertheless remains a formidable fighting force. The capabilities of the ships deployed to the Indian Ocean, for example, are infinitely greater than those which carried the war across the Pacific to Japan and ultimately brought that country to its knees in 1945. Despite advances made by the Soviet Navy since Admiral Sergei G. Gorshkov assumed command in the late 1950s, the American ability to project naval power to distant seas—particularly the Indian Ocean—remains markedly superior to that of the USSR. Given the recent emphasis which Gorshkov has placed on aircraft carrier construction and the development of an amphibious capability, one can conclude that nowhere is the foregoing fact of international life better appreciated than within the walls of the Kremlin. That is not to say, however, that Soviet ability to move large contingents of ground and air forces from the southern portions of the USSR into the Persian Gulf area—where use of the seas is not required—can be effectively countered by American military strength presently in the region.

On the contrary, U.S. armed strength currently stationed in the Indian Ocean is essentially trip-wire in nature. Until Washington is able to deploy far greater military power to the region—permanently, or on extremely short notice—that which is there now will constitute merely a deterrent force. Its presence will do little more than signal to the Soviet Union that any aggressive move on Moscow's part will inevitably raise the distinct risk of confrontation with elements of American military power.

Given the nuclear escalation perils which such a development would entail, the deterrent aspects of current American military deployments to the Indian Ocean are evident. This raises the question of the so-called Rapid Deployment Force (RDF) which the United States has begun to fashion, and what its ultimate materialization will mean for U.S. policy in the Middle East.

If, as advertised, the embryonic RDF eventually evolves into a meaningful ability of the United States to project ground and air power to the region in a timely manner, the ability of the Soviet Union to overrun the region and establish a *fait accompli* before Western—essentially American—power could be brought to bear, would be largely neutralized. The implications for the security of friendly nations in the area are obvious.

8.
The Rapid Deployment Force

WHEN THE underpinnings of American security policy in the Persian Gulf-Indian Ocean area began to crumble with the eruption of the revolution in Iran, followed by the Soviet invasion of Afghanistan, Washington suddenly discovered that its ability to move credible military power into the region, and to do so quickly—either to deter or defeat externally-based aggression—was seriously deficient. Strains on the U.S. Navy, created by the required buildup in the Indian Ocean, were matched by a manifest inability of American Air Force and Army units to reach the area. The entire problem was further exacerbated by a complete absence of bases from which to operate once these forces arrived on the scene. As a result, an earlier Pentagon answer to this kind of international military problem was resurrected and slightly modified.

During the tenure of Robert S. McNamara as U.S. Secretary of Defense, his young systems analysts searched constantly for some means of reducing the size and—of supreme importance—the cost of maintaining the American armed services. The predecessor of the current RDF concept thus came into being in the early 1960s. Essentially, the original notion held that, if a means of placing, in advance, heavy military equipment in any region harboring potential perils for U.S. national interests could be devised, the associated combat personnel could be retained in the continental United States. Then, in the event of trouble, they could be quickly flown to the hot spot in question, together with their personal equipment and weapons, joined to the heavy items already on station—tanks, trucks, mobile artillery, ammunition—and be quickly readied for combat operations. In the jargon of the Pentagon, this concept became known as the Fast Deployment Logistics (FDL) plan.

In accordance with the FDL concept, a number of civilian-manned, air-conditioned cargo ships woud be procured, aboard which heavy equipment for the combat forces would be loaded and maintained in a controlled atmosphere to minimize deterioration during extended storage periods. These ships would then be sailed to potential trouble spots located around the globe where they would wait until the cargoes they carried were needed. For a number of reasons, this program was never implemented. In 1979, however, the idea was dusted off and given a new name, and plans were laid to put it into being. It is important to recognize that, in both instances, the prepositioned equipment ships could be sent to any part of the globe where a potential threat to U.S. interests might arise. In late 1980, the foremost perceived danger lay in the Middle East, specifically in and around the Persian Gulf. For this reason alone, the new U.S. RDF was initially crafted to meet threats to American security evolving in the Indian Ocean region. To understand the aims of this concept, one must examine the present makeup of the RDF, plans for its expansion, and how the resultant military force might ultimately be used.

The Current Anatomy of the RDF

In its initial stages, the RDF was primarily oriented toward prospective crises in the Indian Ocean, and the first ships loaded with prepositioned military equipment reached their holding area at the island base of Diego Garcia in July 1980. Led by the S.S. *American Champion,* seven civilian-manned ships, chartered from U.S. merchant marine owners, commenced sailing from East Coast ports in early July and, by the latter part of August, all were on station in the Indian Ocean. Carrying tanks, armored personnel carriers, self-propelled artillery, and airfield support equipment, the first five ships were joined by one tanker loaded with various types of military fuel and a seventh ship to supply potable water to the troops of the RDF.

The first contingent of RDF troops came from the newly formed 7th Marine Amphibious Brigade, based at the U.S. Marine Corps installation at 29 Palms, California. Personnel were drawn from the 1st Marine Division while their supporting helicopter, fixed-wing aircraft, and logistics elements came from other existing Marine units, mostly on the West Coast of the United States. The 29 Palms site was chosen because it is the Corps' main desert training base.

Airlift for the troops was to be provided, on call, from U.S. Air Force assets assigned to the Military Airlift Command (MAC). The aircraft were initially envisaged as C-5 and C-141 transports in the MAC inventory. Depending on the urgency of movement, it might be deemed necessary for the U.S. Government to commandeer additional aircraft—civilian-owned airliners—from the Civil Reserve Air Fleet (CRAF).

Should it have become necessary to commit the RDF somewhere in the Indian Ocean region during this early period, protection for movement of the prepositioned ships and preliminary close air support for the arriving troops would have been provided by the aircraft carrier battle groups cruising in the Indian Ocean. Once ashore and deployed, a major share of the close air support requirement would be assumed by Air Force and Marine tactical squadrons accompanying the ground elements. As thus configured, the RDF could have been sustained for perhaps two weeks of combat before additional supplies would be needed.

42

Since the present prepositioned ships are standard civilian merchant-men—break-bulk cargo together with so-called roll-on, roll-off types—they need developed port facilities for off-loading. They possess no true amphibious capability. Moreover, it is clear that the incoming aircraft with the Marine brigade or follow-on Army troops could not land against any significant opposition. The airfields to be used would obviously have to be in friendly hands, or they would have to be seized in advance by American military units already in the Indian Ocean. In this connection, one must assume that this would be a prime mission of the 1800-man Navy-Marine amphibious contingent periodically assigned to the Indian Ocean since the initial naval buildup and which is expected to be present most of the time. Marine Lieutenant General Paul X. Kelley, first Com-mander of the Rapid Deployment Joint Task Force—the combined Army, Navy, Air Force, and Marine staff formed on March 1, 1980—claimed that an airborne battalion could be placed in the Persian Gulf region "inside 48 hours, with the entire division following in less than two weeks."[18] At that time, the Joint Task Force command had no forces assigned to its control, but in the event of RDF deployment would have drawn them from existing commands in the various armed services.

This, then, was the structure and status of the Rapid Deployment Force in the closing days of summer 1980. The speed with which the concept was developed—albeit drawing heavily on earlier work with respect to the FDL plan—and initial implementing measures were undertaken is notable. Not since the days of the Vietnam War had American military preparedness seen such swift and comprehensive movement.

By early 1982, significant changes had been made in the RDF, most of them by the new Reagan Administration. On October 1, 1981, the Rapid Deployment Joint Task Force (RDJTF) had been formally chartered as a separate joint command reporting to the President—the National Com-mand Authority—through the Joint Chiefs of Staff (JCS). Furthermore, the commander of the task force had been given actual operational control over several Army units and Air Force tactical squadrons. Fur-thermore, he was accorded access to other forces from which he could draw units in times of crisis. Table 1 lists the potential strength of the RDJTF.

Current and Future Plans for the RDJTF

While the present capabilities of the renamed Rapid Deployment Joint Task Force are admittedly inadequate in the face of any full-scale military

---

[18]Lee Hocksteader, "New Military Unit Hailed by Legion," *Boston Globe*, August 17, 1980, p. 37.

Table 1
Potential Strength of the
Rapid Deployment Joint Task Force

Army
1 Airborne Division
1 Airmobile/Air Assault Division
1 Cavalry Brigade Air Combat (CBAC)
1 Mechanized Infantry Division
Rangers and Unconventional Warfare Units

Marines
1-2 Marine Amphibious Forces (MAF)[a]

Air Force
4-11 Air Force Tactical Fighter Wings (with support air forces)
2 Squadrons of Strategic Bombers (the Strategic Projection Force)

Navy
3 Carrier Battle Groups (CVBGs)
1 Surface Action Group
5 Air-ASW Patrol Squadrons (VP)

Headquarters
1 Army Corps Headquarters
1 Naval Forces Headquarters
1 Air Force Forces Headquarters

---

[a]A MAF typically consists of a reinforced Marine division and a Marine aircraft wing (roughly twice the size of an Air Force tactical fighter wing).

Source: Caspar W. Weinberger, *Annual Report to the Congress, Fiscal Year 1983*, p. III-103

drive by the USSR to seize physical control of the Persian Gulf region and its oil resources, it is nonetheless relevant to other, less severe threats. Recognizing this fact of international life, the Reagan Administration is also pursuing plans to expand these capabilities to the point that a fundamental objective of U.S. Middle East policy can be achieved: maintenance of political stability throughout the region and assured access to the oil resources of the Persian Gulf against all challenges which might be mounted, including any from the Soviet Union.

One of the foremost weaknesses in the concept is the lack of adequate, long-range airlift. Originally, the Lockheed C-141 Starlifter transport could not be refueled in the air. This meant that its range was limited to something on the order of 4,500 miles. The Military Airlift Command's 234 C-141s are currently being modified to lengthen the fuselage and give them an in-flight refueling capability. The conversion—to be completed in 1982—will also increase the plane's load capacity and extend its service life.

The 77 C-5 Galaxy transports, on the other hand, can be fueled in flight. Besides their limited numbers, however, they have experienced serious wing fatigue problems which have appreciably reduced their lift capacity and forced constraints to be imposed on their other operating parameters. Funds are being expended to correct the wing problem as well as to increase load limits from the original 214,000 to 235,000 pounds of cargo by 1987. This aircraft, however, cannot drop cargos by parachute as can the more numerous C-141s and the short-range C-130 Hercules transport.

Even with these improvements, however, the air transport fleet will still be critically short of the necessary aircraft to properly serve the RDJTF concept, especially at maximum distances such as those represented by deployments to the Persian Gulf region. For example, just to move 4 million pounds of cargo and 450 personnel to Egypt in support of one 12-plane F-4 squadron dispatched to train with elements of the Egyptian Air Force, the Military Airlift Command had to commit five C-141s and 28 C-5s. Moreover, this was only the first phase of the airlift. Translated into RDJTF terms—including accompanying fighter and attack aircraft squadrons which would be required—it seems clear that substantial increases in U.S. military air transport capability are urgently required. The need is underscored by Air Force estimates that it would take a minimum of 200 C-141s to carry one fully-equipped airborne brigade on a parachute operation. Since maintenance requirements and other problems would limit the fleet to about 165 aircraft at any given time, the deficiencies are obvious.

To cope with this airlift shortfall the Reagan Administration asked the U.S. Congress—in its 1983 budget submission—for funds to add some 50 new C-5 transports and 44 KC-10 tanker aircraft to the present MAC inventory. The Defense Department has thus shelved any idea of building an entirely new transport—the CX—which had been proposed by President Carter. In the first days of 1982, yet another airlift alternative surfaced on Capitol Hill, one patently driven by local constituent pressures. Few other segments of the American economy—housing and the automobile industry aside—were then suffering as severely as the nation's commercial airlines. As a result, there continued to be an appreciable number of excess, used Boeing 747s which the airlines wanted to rid themselves of, as well as yet others contracted for and under construction. While substantive issues were involved—cost variations inherent in these two alternatives, and questions with regard to loading ease and cargo handling capabilities—it is altogether probable that the final decision will stem more from political than calculated military considerations.

At the same time, it should be recalled that the pioneer seven-ship prepositioning force swinging to its anchors in the Indian Ocean was a similarly *ad hoc,* jury-rigged solution to an acute strategic dilemma. These, after all, were civilian merchant ships lacking any sort of amphibious landing capability. If no adequately equipped port should be immediately available in the event of a crisis, it would be impossible for this force to discharge its cargoes across an open beach, let alone one which might be defended. To overcome this potentially fatal shortcoming, the Carter Administration directed the U.S. Navy to program Service funds— approximately $5 billion—for the design and construction of a series of logistics ships, each specifically to support the RDF. As many as 18 of these special prepositioning ships were envisaged. Under the Carter plan, additional funds would have also been programmed for up to eight high-speed SL-7 cargo ships which could conceivably have cut oceanic transit time from the American East Coast to the Persian Gulf roughly in half.[19]

Finally, the Carter-directed Pentagon five-year plan for protecting U.S. national interests in the Middle East addressed the question of casualties. The U.S. Navy was ordered to earmark money for hospital ships when drawing up its budget proposals covering fiscal years 1982 through 1986. The pertinent directive, signed by Secretary of Defense Harold Brown, called for a minimum of three 250-bed and one 500-bed Selected Reserve-Fleet hospital ships as well as conversion of the passenger liner S.S. *United States* to a hospital ship.[20] Procurement of hospital ships, which disappeared from the U.S. Navy inventory in the aftermath of Vietnam, was then seen as one of the more significant actions being taken by the U.S. Government. It could easily and universally be read as a signal that the new U.S. Rapid Deployment Force, wherever committed, would be prepared and, moreover, determined to shoot, if necessary.

The objective of all these initiatives was eventually to place the RDJTF in a position to move 100,000 to 200,000 combat troops to that distant region quickly enough to forestall a military takeover, even by a concerted Soviet military attack. In the meantime, the Force began exercising its current capabilities in the United States and plans were laid to conduct similar tests at overseas locations.

In August 1980, the Army's 7th Transportation Group checked out its ability to move men and supplies. The 10-day exercise, titled Lifeline 1, involved more than 1,500 soldiers, sailors and Marines, several Navy ships, and a host of truck convoys. Designed to test plans for such movement—"enemy" opposition was included—the exercise was expected to

---

[19]"A Big U.S. Buildup in the Gulf," *Newsweek,* July 14, 1980, p. 30.
[20]George C. Wilson, "U.S. Steps Up Planning for Mideast Bases," *Washington Post,* August 7, 1980, p. A1.

reveal shortcomings and areas requiring various degrees of improvement. These maneuvers followed on the heels of another exercise, one involving troops being trained at Fort Bragg in North Carolina from whence additional elements of the RDJTF could be drawn.

In September 1980, the Carter Administration revealed that plans were afoot to exercise the RDJTF in Egypt in November or December. Expected to be a battalion-size operation, it was then rumored that about 1400 troops—whether Marine or Army was not initially determined—along with their light equipment plus antitank weapons and artillery would be moved from bases in the United States to Ras Banas on the Egyptian Red Sea Coast.[21] Tactical U.S. Air Force units were to be included, flying from the United States to the Cairo West airfield in Egypt as an earlier contingent of fighter aircraft had done. Intended to test the concept and to demonstrate U.S. readiness to react to a crisis in the Persian Gulf region, the trial was expected by observers to include movement of at least some of the prepositioning ships from their holding area at Diego Garcia to Ras Banas. Additionally, such an exercise would signal to the international community that the Force was not only now in being, but that the U.S. Government intended to shape it into a credible tool for use in safeguarding American national interests wherever they might be endangered and the Rapid Deployment Joint Task Force would prove useful.

The overseas RDJTF exercise planned for late 1980 was eventually postponed until the fall of 1981. Commencing in early November of that year, the maneuvers—code-named Bright Star '82—involved the movement of some 4,000 troops by air from the United States to Egypt, vehicles and heavy equipment being landed at Alexandria from U.S. ships. Nonstop flights from the continental United States terminated first in a jump from C-141s by 850 paratroopers on the 14th and a desert bombing run on the 24th by six B-52s. Later in November and during the first week in December, additional phases of the exercise were conducted in Somalia and Oman.[22]

While the performance of the assigned units was impressive, it should be noted that it took a major effort to place some 6,000 personnel in the region, a far cry from the 100,000 to 200,000 that have been discussed since the inception of the RDJTF. There clearly is a very long way to go to bring that concept to fruition.

In the fall of 1982, the government of Egypt declined to permit a second "Bright Star" exercise because of Egyptian opposition to Israeli

---

[21]"U.S. Plans to Fly Troops to Egypt to Test Rapid Deployment Force," *Washington Star*, September 12, 1980, p. 1.
[22]"U.S. Muscle-Flexing," *Time*, November 23, 1981, p. 38.

47

actions in Lebanon. This development underlines the uncertainties facing any U.S. plans for military deployments to the region.

Prospects and Problems in RDJTF Employment

While considerable progress has already been made in transforming a paper plan into a viable capability, questions remain with respect to possible employment of the Force as well to how various technical and political problems associated with the RDJTF will ultimately be resolved. To begin with, no one in Washington is so foolish as to assert that, in the present configuration, it would be a match for a determined Soviet military assault against any state in the Persian Gulf region. Such a claim would patently be incredible. As previously suggested, the general assumption is that for the immediate future the Force will constitute little more than a trip-wire. That is to say, should Moscow seriously contemplate a military incursion anywhere in the area, the Kremlin hierarchy would have to factor into its calculations the very real possibility that Soviet troops and aircraft would swiftly encounter American combat forces.

Deterrence, of course, is the name of this particular game, and caution lies at the very heart of deterrence. If a military or political planner can calculate with relative certainty the risks as opposed to prospective gains in a contemplated military adventure—if uncertainty is largely eliminated—the decision to proceed can be made with minimal trepidation. On the other hand, if that planner cannot be certain whether such an adventure will encounter armed forces from another major power, one capable of inflicting penalties elsewhere around the globe—even if not prohibitive damage in immediate proximity to the aggressive move itself—the decision becomes far more difficult. The element of caution is thus added to the equation and deterrence is enhanced.

Not every U.S. military expert agrees with the trip-wire capacity of the present RDJTF. Retired U.S. Army Colonel John M. Collins, now the respected chief defense analyst with the Congressional Research Service of the Library of Congress, observed that, "The Rapid Deployment Force isn't rapid, and there is not much to deploy." Moreover, he doesn't place much faith in the Force as a deterrent. Recalling that the 400 U.S. soldiers dispatched to make a show of force in 1950 when North Korean troops invaded the South were overrun the very next day, Collins says of those espousing the trip-wire theory, "These guys haven't read their history books. If the Russians ever decide to go for that oil, they won't stop because of a handful of U.S. troops."[23]

---

[23]Michael Getler, "U.S. Moving Fast to Build Up Military Forces in the Persian Gulf," *Washington Post*, August 10, 1980, p. A1.

Collins may be correct in his assessment. Nonetheless, one must take issue with at least one aspect of his analogy. In Korea, troops of the USSR's North Korean surrogate overran the tiny American contingent. Soviet personnel were not involved. In the Kremlin, the leadership certainly assumed—correctly, in light of subsequent events—that the United States would not retaliate directly against the Soviet Union in response to the actions of the North Koreans. As a matter of fact, later in the war, the American Government refused to strike the People's Republic of China, even when combat units of that nation's armed forces entered the Korean War and inflicted disastrous defeats on the United Nations' armies. Had regular Soviet troops faced the prospect of encountering those 400 Americans, the decision to overrun them might have been quite different. One can argue this position with some conviction inasmuch as the United States then still possessed an overwhelming superiority with respect to nuclear weapons. Still, Collins' evaluation cannot be completely discounted.

Criticisms of the RDJTF aside for the moment, there are positive things which can be said about its current capabilities and utility. With the fall of the Shah of Iran, American security policy for the Persian Gulf collapsed and, as was the case with the United Kingdom's military withdrawal from the region in 1971, an unquestioned power vacuum again developed. Protestations of regional states within the Gulf that the Soviet Union would not attempt to fill such a void so long as the United States made no move to do so are not convincing; history teaches that this is neither a valid nor a prudent assumption. In view of Moscow's actions elsewhere since the end of World War II—Eastern Europe, Iran, the Korean Peninsula, Ethiopia, Angola—it stretches credibility to expect that the Kremlin could resist the temptation to replace Western influence in the Persian Gulf. Especially in light of projected Soviet needs for oil to supply itself and its East European client states in the future, it is only realistic to postulate that Moscow would find a politically unstable and powerless Persian Gulf to be an irresistible target. Thus, the foremost case which can be made for the RDJTF is that, to an extent, it fills the international power vacuum created by the Iranian revolution and, thereby, attenuates any temptation for the Soviets to move in. As the strength and credibility of the Rapid Deployment Joint Task Force expand, such lures for the USSR should be further reduced.

There are other useful purposes to which the Force can be put, including reassurance of friends and allies in the region. These nations watched with growing alarm as political conditions throughout the area deteriorated in recent years, and the United States appeared not only unwilling but incapable of doing anything about it. Stretching back to the final

49

American retreat from Vietnam, a long series of international crises in which Washington has been perceived by the world community as timid, weak and vacillating—Angola, the Horn of Africa, Iran, Soviet troops in Cuba—generated an international image of America as a "crippled giant." Consequently, the value of U.S. commitment and determination has inevitably been called into serious question.

This growing perception played a prime role in the less-than-enthusiastic reception which U.S. offers of aid received in Islamabad following the Soviet invasion of Afghanistan. Understandably, General Zia did not want to risk the predictable, savage Soviet reaction which might be prompted by receipt of direct military aid from the United States, unless its character added measurably to Pakistan's armed strength. It seems clear that, in his view, the amount and character of the assistance initially offered by the Carter Administration—especially in view of the probability that the United States would refuse to come to Pakistan's aid in the event of a Soviet invasion—simply could not offset the danger of provoking Moscow.

In some measure, the development and deployment of the first elements of the RDJTF and the periodic exercising of its capabilities will serve to restore a portion of the lost confidence in the will and reliability of the United States. One can be quite certain, for instance, that these events are being watched carefully in Saudi Arabia. Moreover, despite their public "pox on both your houses" stance, one suspects that the realists within government circles of the Persian Gulf shaikhdoms view the situation in a similar light. As the capability of the Force increases, such perceptions are likely to gain greater currency.

Further, it is not just in the Indian Ocean area that the effects of a relevant and credible RDJTF will be felt. One of the foremost failings of American foreign policy formulation lies in an almost chronic inability to look for, let alone identify, ramifications which actions in one part of the globe may have half a world away. In this connection, it is important to remember that the Rapid Deployment Joint Task Force is designed to be *mobile.* While it is currently oriented toward the Indian Ocean and the Persian Gulf, it could just as well be utilized in a contingency situation anywhere else. Nations in other parts of the world are undoubtedly following its progress, evaluating its usefulness in their regions, and drawing appropriate conclusions from their findings. Its successes or failures could well have significant impact in many distant areas encompassing vital U.S. interests.

Still another purpose which could conceivably be served by the RDJTF would be the rendering of assistance to some friendly nation suddenly beset with external aggression launched by a country other than the Soviet Union. Such a possibility is not exactly alien to the Persian Gulf.

For example, immediately following London's grant of full independence to Kuwait in 1961, Iraq—citing the precedent set by the Ottoman Empire—resurrected an old claim to sovereignty over all of the shaikhdom. Menacing troop movements on the Iraqi side of the frontier suggested that Baghdad meant to take advantage of dwindling British power within the Gulf and Kuwait's increasingly exposed position. As the pressure on the shaikhdom mounted, and other Arab states made no urgent moves to come to its assistance, Shaikh Abdullah—then the ruler of Kuwait—appealed to the United Kingdom for help. British troops from the lower Gulf, accompanied by warships and aircraft, arrived on the scene swiftly and Iraq abruptly decided not to seize what had initially appeared to be a golden opportunity. Ultimately, the British forces, which landed in July, were replaced by a pan-Arab contingent belatedly collected and deployed in September.

It would be in situations such as this that the RDJTF, on invitation from the threatened country, could be employed to preserve stability in the region and avoid eruption of a local conflagration which might play havoc with the flow of oil from the Gulf. In these circumstances, it conceivably could require little more than movement of a U.S. carrier battle group to the waters of the imperiled nation to damp down the crisis. The implicit backup provided by the Rapid Deployment Joint Task Force, featuring its greater ground force capability as compared with that of the normally integral Marine amphibious troops of the American Indian Ocean fleet, would further underline American support.

As for possible intervention in internal, clearly domestic upheavals, it is difficult to envision any U.S. forces being committed in the absence of a strong, public appeal from the ruling government, such as that issued by Lebanon in 1982. Even in such circumstances, the United States Government would have to weigh with extreme care any decision to become directly involved. Included among the myriad factors which would have to be considered would be political reactions, not only within the country itself—where the presence of American military forces might further complicate ongoing problems of the ruling government—but those of adjacent nations as well. It will be recalled that the British intervention in Kuwait in 1961 did not meet with universal Arab applause, despite the fact that an appeal for help had been sent to London by the legitimate Kuwaiti Government.

The initial technical and military complications associated with the budding RDJTF remain formidable. Deficiencies such as those in airlift capacity, shortages of skilled soldiers and sailors, inadequate numbers of proper prepositioning ships, and other difficulties combined, at the outset, to cast serious doubts on the relevance and credibility of the Rapid

Deployment Joint Task Force. In addition to the foregoing problems, there are significant political ones as well.

From the beginning, officials in the Pentagon have claimed they are satisfied that necessary overflight and landing rights to accommodate the RDJTF will be readily forthcoming. Whether the question centers on initial deployment or the movement of subsequent reinforcements, these officials assert that en route stops for fuel and rest between the United States and the Indian Ocean—via the Mediterranean or the Pacific—"would not be a problem."[24] Yet, international political scar tissue from similar U.S. attempts since 1973 offers abundant testimony to the thesis that, on the contrary, such clearances will most certainly pose severe, perhaps insurmountable, complications.

As noted, in 1973 only Portugal—among all of America's presumably close NATO allies—permitted use of its territory by the massive airlift mounted to resupply Israel during the fourth Middle East war. In 1979, the U.S. decision to send a squadron of fighter aircraft to Saudi Arabia to demonstrate support for the Kingdom following the Iranian revolution provided a second humiliating example. Spanish actions stemmed from an incredible political gaffe on the part of the United States: failure to procure permission for the planes to land and refuel at the American-leased air base at Torrejon before the planned operation was publicly announced. On the basis of these experiences, one would expect any prudent U.S. defense planner to assume that transit facilities would probably *not* be available at the precise time they would be most urgently required.

A second problem is of lesser but nonetheless substantial dimensions: There presently are no locations in the Indian Ocean where the RDJTF can be exercised. Throughout the Second World War, especially prior to every major amphibious campaign in the Pacific, projected landings were rehearsed in full detail before the actual assault was undertaken. It can be argued that this sort of full-scale preliminary is not necessarily required for the RDJTF, although the abortive U.S. attempt to rescue its diplomatic hostages in Iran suggests rather strongly that any assault force should rehearse thoroughly in advance, and with the weapons and equipment it actually intends to use in the event it is committed to action. The troops of the Rapid Deployment Joint Task Force, of course, can be given general training in the United States.

Still, it is vitally important that even the present prepositioning ships go through the process of off-loading, exercising, and then back-loading the equipment they carry, if for no other reason than to learn how it can

---

[24]*Ibid.*

best be done and to uncover unforeseen problems which it is essential to avoid in a combat situation. Moreover, normal rotation of personnel in the various ships' companies demands that such exercises be conducted periodically. Once amphibious-capable prepositioning ships become a part of the RDJTF inventory, it will then be necessary similarly to exercise them in over-the-beach operations with the myriad tasks being carried out by those personnel who would have to accomplish them in an instant crisis. Perhaps by the time such ships are available, these kinds of training facilities will be available. At the moment, they are not.

Even Sultan Qaboos of Oman, who placed himself in an exceedingly exposed political position with respect to the rest of the Arab states when he signed a facilities-use agreement with the United States, is moving cautiously. For example, when he was briefed on U.S. plans for the RDJTF exercise, Bright Star 82, he insisted on a dramatic reduction in the scale of the Oman portion of the operation and forbade any Western press coverage of the proposed landings on Masirah Island. In this instance, traditional U.S. policy with respect to the marathon Arab-Israeli dispute predictably intruded. In a recent interview, Youseff Alawi, Oman's Minister of State for Foreign Affairs, said, "The United States needs to cooperate with the Arab countries to prevent Soviet expansionism. The primary way is to look to the Middle East problem and the Palestinian issue. That would ease the whole thing and change the whole picture for many Arab countries to cooperate [with the United States] rather freely."[25]

---

[25]David B. Ottaway, "Oman Expects U.S. Help for Use of Its Bases," *Washington Post*, April 7, 1982, p. A1.

9.
Initial Actions
of the Reagan Administration

I T IS OBVIOUS that one of the more salutary effects of the Soviet invasion
of Afghanistan was the belated awakening of the Carter Administration to the Kremlin's imperialist ambitions. Whether this sort of realization also penetrated the ken of the Japanese and the citizens of Western
Europe, however, remains problematical. Although all of the countries
these people inhabit are far more dependent upon the petroleum resources
of the region than is the United States, their governments seem to be far
less concerned with the problem than they ought to be, and far more
reluctant to make the hard choices which their survival demands than
was even the U.S. Government under the leadership of President Carter.

With the American election of 1980 and assumption of the Presidency
by Ronald Reagan, a major shift in U.S. military policy was signaled to
the world. Pledged to reverse past trends which had dramatically reduced
the nation's military power, Reagan immediately began to move in that
direction. By January of 1982, when the Administration submitted the
first Defense Department budget which it could call exclusively its own,
the details emerged.

To begin with, it was obvious that international maritime realities had
at last been recognized. Secretary of Defense Caspar W. Weinberger
stated in his 1982 submission to the Congress: "Our primary goal is to
establish and maintain maritime superiority over any likely enemy, taking
due account of both his allies and ours."[26] He recommended dramatic
increases in the Navy, particularly in those portions of the naval shipbuilding program devoted to the projection of striking power on a global
basis. Advertised as a major shift in national strategy, the budget nevertheless appeared to be flawed in two respects.

First, it continued heavy emphasis and spending on the American
ground force contribution to the defense of Western Europe. Given the
difficulties then besetting the U.S. economy, it seemed clear that the huge
defense increases proposed would encounter stiff opposition in the Congress. If the envisaged naval buildup was to survive, extensive cuts would
have to be made elsewhere in the U.S. military budget. The most likely
candidate was the Army and its massive ground force commitment to

---

[26]Caspar W. Weinberger, Secretary of Defense, *Annual Report to the Congress, Fiscal Year 1983*, p. III-19.

NATO, a burden which many Americans increasingly believed the Europeans themselves should be carrying.

Second, the Reagan five-year naval shipbuilding plan was heavily oriented toward large and expensive ships, predominantly carriers, cruisers and attack submarines. (See Appendix A.) The 1983 budget and subsequent projections obviously provided inadequate funds for those less capable and less expensive ships—destroyers, mobile logistic support and amphibious ships—which were clearly needed in large numbers if the United States was to counter the growing global challenge being posed by the expanded outreach of the Soviet Navy. Only by cutting back on the planned production of high-technology ships can needed numbers of those less expensive ones, which can safely operate in areas of minimal naval threat around the world, be acquired.

As for the Rapid Deployment Joint Task Force, the first wholly Reagan budget made no significant changes in its composition other than to cancel the previously cited CX transport program in favor of additional purchases of existing aircraft. On the other hand, it made major organizational changes. In his report, Secretary Weinberger stressed regional threats and a newly-narrowed focus of the RDJTF:

> The continuing Soviet occupation of Afghanistan, the Iran-Iraq War, Arab-Israeli disputes in southern Lebanon, the conflict between North and South Yemen, and the Iranian attacks on Kuwaiti oil facilities exemplify the range of regional instabilities that complicate our policy and strategy....
> On October 1, 1981, we chartered the RDJTF [Rapid Deployment Joint Task Force] to be a separate joint task force reporting directly to the National Command Authority (NCA) through the Joint Chiefs of Staff (JCS). Furthermore, the Commander, RDJTF, is now assigned operational planning responsibility for SWA [South West Asia] only. This narrowed scope reflects our recognition of the need for a fulltime major commander to develop detailed plans for the wide range of possible contingencies in the region."[27]

Moreover, for the first time, the new Administration gave the RDJTF commander actual operational control of assigned combat units whereas, previously, his organization comprised only the personnel of his planning staff. Several Army units and Air Force tactical fighter squadrons now report directly to him. (See page 44 for the major types of combat forces available to the RDJTF.)

The unilateral actions which have been taken by the United States, along with those it clearly plans to implement in the future, are important. Still, it is imperative that Washington also press its principal allies to participate actively in stemming the Soviet Middle East drive.

---

[27]*Ibid.*, pp. III-101 to 103.

10.
The Current Geostrategic Situation in the Middle East

E VEN A CURSORY examination of the Middle East, particularly beyond Suez, reveals that the evident Soviet drive to achieve hegemony over the Persian Gulf region and its petroleum reserves is well advanced. Begun in Egypt and next spilling over into the Sudan, Moscow's continuing campaign has been aimed at fashioning a noose around the entire Arabian Peninsula and the Gulf. Ubiquitous Soviet "Treaties of Friendship and Cooperation" have, over the years, been signed with Iraq, India, South Yemen, Somalia and Ethiopia. Despite latter-day reverses which Moscow has suffered in Egypt, the Sudan and Somalia, the noose is nonetheless nearly complete. Replacement of Somalia by Ethiopia, as the southwestern segment, must be considered a net gain by the USSR. Not only do military facilities in the latter country now extend the Soviet clamp on the Red Sea all the way to the southern entrance of the Suez Canal, but they provide a high road for subversion into the central portion of the African continent. Further, a commanding position just outside the Bab el Mandeb—once guaranteed by the base at Berbera— is still available to the Soviet Navy through continuing access to even better facilities at Aden.

In geostrategic terms, only two striking gaps remain in the loop. The first is Oman. Although the Soviet-backed Dhofar rebellion was ultimately put down by Sultan Qaboos—with British, Jordanian and Iranian assistance—one must deem that particular insurrection to be quiescent rather than moribund. Should the revolt be reactivated, perhaps with Cuban and East German help this time, the Omani monarch would find himself in even more desperate straits. No longer can he realistically look to the British for aid and, certainly, he cannot expect any help from Iran. The only pledge he could conceivably rely on is that from the late Anwar Sadat: to provide troops and equipment if the rebels become active again. How Hosni Mubarak stands is unknown. Nor is it known if the recently concluded agreement for use of facilities by the United States contains any sort of American commitment, explicit or implicit.

One can readily assume that Sultan Qaboos did not overlook the distinct possibility that even limited numbers of American military personnel stationed in his country—albeit clothed in civilian garb—would provide a sort of protective U.S. military aura and thereby enhance his country's internal security. As has been previously suggested by the American

56

experience in Korea, surrogate actions are not necessarily deterred in this fashion. It seems probable that a publicly proclaimed guarantee from the United States would better serve the purpose in that it would be more likely to forestall the sort of miscalculation made by Kim Il Sung in the wake of Secretary Acheson's fateful speech.

On the opposite side of the Persian Gulf lies the second remaining gap in the Soviet noose: Iran. As knowledgeable observers predicted from the start, the Iranian Revolution is going through only its first stage. The anti-Shah banner, raised by the Ayatollah Ruhollah Khomeini, attracted a supremely unlikely collection of conspirators. It was obvious from the onset of political troubles in Iran that once their initial objective had been achieved—destruction of the monarchy—disparate elements making up the revolutionary forces would begin to fractionate and that a long and bitter struggle for power would ensue. That this is precisely what is happening is beyond question.

Iran clearly remains in turmoil, domestic unrest is prevalent, and various factions seeking everything from local autonomy to either full independence or complete national control are busily working to achieve their objectives. The patriotic upwelling which attended the war with Iraq must be considered temporary. Historically, dictatorial regimes in power—when their rule has come under domestic fire—have sought to deflect the pressures emanating from internal opposition by conjuring up a menace from some outside source. In the Iranian case, Iraq fortuitously provided such a diversion. One should expect these internal forces to begin warring anew in Iran once the Iraqi threat is dissipated one way or another.

That the Soviet Union is covertly supporting those Iranian elements friendly to Moscow is also beyond doubt. How the issue will eventually be resolved is, at present, anyone's guess. For example, it would be foolish to rule out Soviet pursuit of the Afghan model in Iran. That is to say, the Teheran government may face still further descent into political chaos, including possible seizure of power by Marxist elements and subsequent issuance of an "invitation" for armed forces of the USSR to intervene to help "preserve order" and, ostensibly, to prevent "outside" forces from subverting the "legitimate" government of the "Iranian people." In this regard, the latest regime, still headed by Khomeini but featuring more pliable presidents, is frequently referred to in some circles as the "second Kerensky" government in Iran.

As implied by the obvious Soviet effort to subvert the entire region, political instability is a fundamental threat in the Middle East. In this regard, Iran clearly presents a companion danger to the status quo by its efforts to export the kind of fundamentalist Moslem revolution which Khomeini brought to that nation. Certainly, one can reasonably assume that a primary motivation for the Iraqi invasion of Iran stemmed from the knowledge that Khomeini harbored retributory designs against the regime of Saddam Hussein. The Ayatollah never forgave the Baghdad Government for expelling him in October 1978 after he had spent 14 years of exile in Najjaf. Hussein, meanwhile, is uncomfortably aware that he rules a country whose population is 95 percent Moslem, the majority of them Shiite—the dominant religious sect in Iran—while he and his entourage are Sunni Moslems.

Another country which has recently baked in the hot blast of this sort of religious upheaval is the tiny shaikhdom of Bahrain. There, a plot was uncovered during the closing days of 1981 aimed at the overthrow of the Sunni ruling family, the al-Khalifa. The Iranian hand was clearly revealed, and Teheran's reasoning is not difficult to divine. The population of Bahrain is about equally divided between Sunni and Shiite Moslems. Since the bulk of the Bahrain Shiites are rural, while the Sunnis predominate in the urban areas, this shaikhdom must have seemed to Khomeini eminently ripe for the very sort of revolt he had been able to foment in Iran. In Bahrain, Khomeini failed. What the future will bring, as is the case with Iraq, is uncertain. Moreover, this obvious threat of domestic instability haunts all of the Arab states on the Arabian Peninsula and has been greatly exacerbated by the Iranian counter-invasion of Iraq, although the ultimate outcome of this effort is still in doubt.

It will be recalled that Shiites in the Eastern Province of Saudi Arabia—where the major oil fields are located—recently responded to Khomeini's siren call. Since they constitute only a small minority in a predominantly Sunni nation, their political activities could normally be ignored. Their location, however, makes a very large difference in the international petroleum equation.

Thus, threats to Western interests in the Middle East materialize on two levels. First is the menace presented by the expansionistic aims of the Soviet Union. This, in turn, is dual-faceted: the possibility of (1) an overt Soviet invasion of the region—most unlikely—and (2) Moscow-sponsored subversion—a continuing prospect. Second, the regional revolutionary religious threat posed by Iranian Shiites under the direction of the Ayatollah Khomeini as well as by other radicals, such as those who seized the Grand Mosque in Mecca in 1979 and assassinated Sadat in 1981, persists.

Geopolitical problems for the United States are not, to be sure, confined to the region "East of Suez." On the Mediterranean side of that canal, there is Colonel Muammar al-Qadhafi, in religious terms a close compatriot of Khomeini. Qadhafi, from the moment he instigated the coup which overthrew King Idris, has been a troublesome thorn in the American international hide. It should be recalled that, shortly after Qadhafi seized power in 1969, he ejected the United States from the all-important Wheelus Air Force Base in Libya. Since that time, the Libyan strongman has pursued an intense campaign against Israel, American policy in the Middle East, and, lately, the United States itself. The most recent manifestation of the Colonel's ire materialized in the Gulf of Sirte (Khalij Surt). Drawing a line across the Gulf—from the northern-most projection of Libya into the Mediterranean Sea to the western promontory near Tripoli, Colonel Qadhafi claims that all waters within this line belong to his nation. This, of course, is in clear violation of established international law. Confrontation came in August of 1981.

Early on the morning of August 26, a main element of the U.S. Sixth Fleet, specifically Task Force 60, was conducting a missile exercise between 60 and 100 miles north of the Libyan coastline. This was well beyond internationally recognized Libyan territorial waters—even the Soviet Union does not recognize the claims Qadhafi makes to the Gulf of Sirte—and selected because of the low density of shipping and civilian air traffic. Numerous Libyan aircraft had followed the exercise the day before, retiring as soon as they were intercepted by Task Force 60's combat air patrols. Early on Wednesday morning, however, they did not depart. When a pair of U.S. F-14 fighters approached them, the pilot of one Libyan SU-22 launched a Soviet-made Atoll missile. It missed. The F-14s quickly evaded, swung around and, firing heat-seeking Sidewinder missiles, promptly shot down both Libyan planes. The incident lasted less than a minute, the reverberations much longer.

International reaction to the U.S. response was mixed. The main unknown was what would happen in the future. Qadhafi threatened war against the United States if the Sixth Fleet penetrated the Gulf of Sirte again. It was just as clear that the United States, to prevent Libya's claim becoming recognized customary international law, would ply those waters in the future. When another incident might occur and what the result might be were the fundamental questions.

This, then, is the geostrategic complexion of the Middle East in the early 1980s. As can be seen, while the term "Middle East" describes a general region which most informed people comprehend, it is nonetheless an area of infinite complexity—geographic as well as political and religious. Moreover, it is into this highly uncertain environment that the U.S. armed forces have been directed to move and in which they may be forced to fight to protect the vital interests of their countrymen.

Should Iran ultimately emerge from its political travail with a radical leftist or a truly Marxist government of the Ethiopian type, the Soviet campaign for dominion over nations of the Arabian Gulf will assuredly have taken a major step forward. Once the region is ringed with Marxist-oriented client states, Moscow's ability to exert irresistible political pressure on the remaining countries of the region would be enormous, and complete domination within easy reach. One is compelled to note that this prospect should be haunting every one of the remaining royal rulers on the Arabian Peninsula.

In such a context, it is also difficult to understand Arab calls for American military withdrawal from the Northwest Indian Ocean and Persian Gulf. It can only be explained, one supposes, as deriving from an exceedingly naive belief that, should this transpire, Moscow would benignly emulate the American example. History, of course, is littered with the wreckage of states which have espoused such an idealistic view of actions that large powers may take vis-a-vis smaller ones.

Protestations of idealists notwithstanding, we all live in a power-political world, and modern nation-states ignore this fact of international life at their extreme peril. Idealism, when permitted to govern dealings between countries, is nothing more than a prescription for national disaster. No one underlined the validity of this assertion more succinctly than did the late dictator of the Soviet Union, Joseph Stalin. When cautioned by President Roosevelt that Allied leaders would have to take into account the views of the Pope in Rome, Stalin derisively asked, "How many divisions does the Pope have?" Rulers in and around the Persian Gulf, who publicly demand removal of American military power from the region, would do well to frame this power-political quote and hang it on their office walls.

11.
Attitudes of Other
Extra-Regional Powers

SIGNIFICANT ACTORS in the Middle East drama are not limited to the littoral nations themselves, the United States or the Soviet Union. Countries of Western Europe, a large number of Third World states, and the foremost nations in the Western Pacific have a vital stake in maintenance of political stability in the Middle East. How these governments react, individually or collectively, to threats posed from whatever source can produce a decisive impact. For this reason alone, it is important to examine the energy positions of some of these countries together with their views with respect to the excruciating problems confronting political and economic stability in the Middle East.

West European Attitudes and American Actions in the Middle East

In general, the attitudes of West European nations toward the Middle East flow from two imperatives. To begin with, they are heavily dependent on Persian Gulf oil, in 1981 importing almost eight million barrels per day. While the United States concurrently looked to the Gulf for a little more than 20 percent of its annual petroleum imports, the figure for the West Europeans—the United Kingdom and Norway aside, thanks to North Sea discoveries and exploitation—was closer to 70 percent. Thus held hostage to oil produced by Middle East nations, Europeans have been understandably unwilling to embrace policies which would earn them any significant disfavor in the Arab world. Moreover, many members of the North Atlantic Alliance, particularly those in Northern Europe, have traditionally exhibited a strong reluctance to become involved in international crises lying beyond the formal defensive boundaries the North Atlantic Alliance established at its inception. Taken together, these factors have governed West European attitudes toward the Middle East and toward associated U.S. policies for more than three decades.

The significance of these reactions lies in the impact they have had on Western defense efforts—at the moment primarily American—to stem the clearly evident Soviet drive for control of Middle East oil. Given the actions of NATO nations to date—more precisely, the lack thereof—it appears that most of these countries are content to watch the United States go the course alone, without any of them having to contribute money, military forces or political capital to safeguard what must be considered vital interests of their own. Until recent months, this attitude characterized all NATO nations except France and the United Kingdom. These two were briefly joined by the Federal Republic of Germany when it sent a tiny naval force into the Indian Ocean in the early days of 1980. Incidentally, this deployment marked the first time since the days of World War II that German warships have appeared in waters beyond the North Atlantic and, other than as a part of NATO's Standing Naval Force Atlantic, the Mediterranean.

As for the balance of West European countries, it is obvious that historical proclivities still govern. When the North Atlantic Alliance was founded in 1949, all of these nations were delighted to have the United States—with its then-dominant nuclear weaponry—at their side. It seemed clear to them that they would only have to make a token commitment to their own conventional defense and their national security would be preserved. After all, the giant across the Atlantic possessed an overwhelming advantage with respect to this awesome new weapon, and Moscow would not dare test West European defenses when such action might conceivably call down on its head a Damoclean nuclear sword. Feeling secure under this atomic umbrella, these countries traded comparatively modest contributions to their own conventional defense for American, British and French commitments to guard the formal boundaries of the Alliance.

From the outset, however, these same allies adamantly opposed any Alliance move which might commit them to action—political or military—beyond those limits. With the British and French empires not yet totally dissolved and American involvement extending worldwide, most NATO member states demanded ironclad restraints on extra-regional Alliance responsibilities. Even the Belgians—with their colonial holdings in Central Africa still intact—and the Dutch—struggling to hold on in Indonesia and New Guinea—were unwilling to trade possible entanglements outside Europe for the benefits of American nuclear protection. Consequently, this attitude became cemented in the North Atlantic condominium. It remains so to the present.

So ingrained has this stance become that, when growing West European dependence on the oil of the Middle East began to penetrate the consciousness of these nations, they still vociferously objected to any changes in NATO's defensive boundaries. Adhering tenaciously to the Tropic of Cancer as the outermost Atlantic maritime frontier of the Alliance, they steadfastly refused to discuss any alteration. Despite entreaties of other member states—especially requests from the United States—or those of NATO's military commanders, these member states stolidly maintained their opposition to any change in those defensive boundaries.

62

Thus, today, no forces operating under the collective NATO banner are permitted to cross the originally established limits. Despite their growing dependence on the Middle East, the attitudes of European nations remain embedded in the concrete of the past.

Acting unilaterally, some countries have undertaken various initiatives to safeguard their national interests beyond the Alliance's boundaries—most notably, France and the United Kingdom. This is not surprising, given the colonial positions they still held, at the time NATO was formed, along the East African coast and throughout the remainder of the Indian Ocean. The most extensive colonial retreat, of course, was executed by London.

Exhausted by the effort to defeat Hitler and his Nazi legions, beset with the fiscal and military burdens associated with trying to hold together a crumbling empire in the face of a rising tide of nationalism, the British Labour Government announced in 1968 that it intended to liquidate all of its military commitments "East of Suez" in the years just ahead. Originally, the notion was gradually to withdraw the nation's military forces in a phased plan to be implemented between the date of the announcement and 1977. Before the first elements could be brought home, however, a second declaration let it be known that the final date would be 1971. It therefore became obvious that, unless some other Western power moved to compensate for the proposed British action, a power vacuum would inexorably materialize in the critical northwest quadrant of the Indian Ocean, particularly in the Persian Gulf. Only the British commitment to Sultan Qaboos of Oman provided an exception subsequent to execution in 1971 of the declared British policy. With the ultimate defeat of the Dhofari rebels in 1975, even that British commitment essentially came to an end. One must conclude that, even if the Dhofar rebellion were to be reactivated today, the likelihood of substantial, direct British military support for the Sultan falls somewhere between remote and nonexistent.

As for the French, the government in Paris presents a unique case insofar as Western Europe is concerned. One of the obvious aims of the De Gaulle foreign policy was maintenance of influence throughout France's old empire—particularly among those colonies granted independence—as well as retaining military access to facilities in those fledgling countries. In pursuing this aim, he and his successors have been strikingly successful, especially in the Indian Ocean. Despite the receding tide of empire, the French Navy today enjoys access to former colonial ports in Djibouti and Reunion, as well as to others in non-French countries such as Mauritius, the Seychelles and Kenya. Moreover, French warships, thanks to that nation's support of the Arabs during the 1973 Middle East war, are frequent callers in Arab ports throughout the northwest quadrant of the

Indian Ocean. Altogether, it can be fairly said that the French—whether in the Francophone zones of Central Africa or throughout the Indian Ocean—have managed to preserve many military footholds so necessary to maintenance of French influence.

The foregoing discussion leads to a fundamental question for the United States as it seeks to insure stability in the Persian Gulf region. Given the manifest difficulties created for the already thinly-spread U.S. armed forces by escalating demands in the Indian Ocean, can the United States expect any sort of military assistance from its allies?

As for action under the banner of the North Atlantic Alliance, the answer seems to be an emphatic no. Given NATO's track record over more than three decades in failing to meet its responsibilities for the military defense of Western Europe, it is altogether unlikely that NATO's member states will expend the necessary additional monies to place any sort of military force in the Indian Ocean on a collective basis. This, then, raises a secondary issue. Barring direct military contributions beyond the Alliance's boundaries, formally defined in 1949, will these Allies undertake to compensate—in the West European theater—for selected withdrawal of American military units being deployed to the Indian Ocean? While less emphatic than the foregoing response, this one must generally be considered negative as well. Previously cited governmental reluctance to meet military readiness goals for the joint defense of their own national borders suggests that West European capitals would not look favorably on still further expenditures to compensate for American forces withdrawn to cope with extra-regional challenges to NATO interests. Within the North Atlantic Alliance there are, of course, individual national exceptions.

The Federal Republic of Germany (FRG) has indicated, by its aforementioned naval deployment to the Indian Ocean region, that Bonn recognizes the overall West European stake in the Persian Gulf. Moreover, a significant change in the post-World War II agreements which have constrained West German rearmament has recently been effected. The seven-nation Western European Union (WEU)—Great Britain, France, Italy, Belgium, Holland, Luxembourg and West Germany—voted in 1980 to rescind the naval building restrictions the Union originally imposed on Bonn when West Germany was admitted to membership in 1955.[28] Setting limits of 3,000 tons on the size of warships and 1,800 tons on that of submarines the Germans could build, the Union had sought to insure that any new German fleet would possess little more than coastal defense capabilities. Moreover, the WEU nations insisted, within the NATO con-

---

[28]"W. Germans Get OK for Expanded Navy," *Washington Star,* July 22, 1980, p. 12.

text, that FRG warships be restricted to operations in the Baltic Sea rather than in the open waters of the North Atlantic Ocean. Bonn itself supplemented those supposed safeguards by arbitrarily confining its naval craft to regions lying within 24-hours steaming time of home waters, or approved NATO sea areas. All of these constraints have now been lifted.

Given the long lead-time involved in modern warship construction, no dramatic increase in the size of the Federal German Navy is imminent. The recent Bonn offer to deploy its ships into the North Sea-North Cape-Iceland triangle, however, has been accepted by its NATO allies. Such action will release some small American and British naval elements (destroyer and submarine types) for deployment to the Indian Ocean and the Mediterranean Sea. Beyond this, any significant naval assistance from the Germans is several years away.

As for help in the Indian Ocean region, the only realistic prospects are assistance from Great Britain and France, and these are not great. Under the leadership of Margaret Thatcher—confronted by mammoth economic ills—defense spending by Britain has encountered heavy seas. Particularly hard hit has been the Royal Navy where a mandated 25 percent reduction has forced halts in ongoing and projected construction as well as some warship decommissionings. Except for those few ships still building in the United Kingdom, further improvement cannot be considered a near-term possibility.[29]

Developments in recent times—in response to the Iraq-Iran war, for instance—have provided encouraging clues with respect to Western attitudes toward the region. Especially following the Iranian threat to block the Strait of Hormuz, Great Britain and France moved swiftly to emphasize their naval presences in the region. In early October 1980, in addition to the 31 American warships then operating in the northwest quadrant of the Indian Ocean, France had some 20 men-o'-war and the British had sent a destroyer and an oiler.[30] Moreover, there were reports that allied pressures on Germany were growing for a similar show of interest by Bonn. This transpired despite the sensitivity with which such a move was viewed by former German Chancellor Helmut Schmidt. In his campaign for reelection in 1980, he repeatedly asserted that the German

---

[29]It is possible that the seizure of the Falkland Islands by Argentina in the early days of April 1982—revealing as it most certainly did the current decrepit state of the Royal Navy—may reverse present trends in the United Kingdom. Moreover, one would be exceedingly naive to think that the Spanish—observing continuing British possession of Gibraltar—were not following ongoing events in the South Atlantic and contemplating similar action in the not-too-distant future. How London could withstand successfully a second assault on those minuscule overseas holdings which have survived the postwar tide of nationalism, given the depleted state of the Royal Navy, beggars credibility.

[30]George C. Wilson, "Iraq-Bound Soviet Ships Turn Back Still Loaded," *Washington Post*, October 2, 1980, p. 1.

Constitution rules out any movement of West German armed forces outside the formal geographic boundaries of the Atlantic Alliance.[31]

The Nations of the Pacific Far East

Comparatively little has appeared in American print, or elsewhere, with respect to either the attitudes or the policies of nations in the Western Pacific toward the Middle East. The major actors in that part of the world—Australia, New Zealand, China and Japan—nonetheless have enormous interests in what is happening in South Asia. Japan, in particular, is exceedingly dependent on Persian Gulf oil. But the Japanese suffer under the restrictions of an American-imposed national constitution which was designed, in the period immediately following World War II, to insure against any revival of militarism in that country. Accordingly, the Japanese Maritime Self-Defense Force has minimal capability to defend Japan's shores, not to mention projecting that limited power beyond the nation's boundaries.

In the case of Japan, as with that of Western Europe, the odds presently are prohibitively high against Tokyo making any military contribution to maintaining stability in the Persian Gulf and the Indian Ocean. About the best that can be hoped for is assumption by the Japanese Maritime Self-Defense Force of a greater role in guarding the sea lanes running along the rim of the Pacific Far East. Even in this instance there are acute problems. Despite the years which have elapsed and the healing accomplished since the end of the Second World War, a good deal of scar tissue—generated by Japanese conduct during that brutal conflict—still exists. The Japanese themselves are extremely sensitive to this situation and cannot, therefore, be expected to authorize their naval forces to stray far from home waters, despite mounting calls from most of the countries in the region for Japan to undertake a far larger role in regional security.

Here one finds the main discrepancy between conditions in Western Europe and those in the Pacific Far East. In Europe, there is the North Atlantic Alliance. An association comprising most nations in Western Europe, it was able to take a collective decision and, speaking with a single voice, invite a recent enemy—West Germany—to rearm and thereby contribute to the common defense. By contrast, no such comparable organization has ever been established in the Far East. There is no similar concerted voice available to enlist a former enemy—in this instance, Japan—in the collective defense of the Far East region.

---

[31]John Vinocur, "Bonn Expecting Allied Pressure to Send Navy Force to Gulf," *New York Times*, October 13, 1980, p. 16.

Australia, too, has an important stake in Persian Gulf and Indian Ocean stability. The Fraser Government in Canberra was enraged by President Carter's unilateral offer, made shortly after he took office in 1977, to negotiate with the Soviet Union a complete demilitarization of the Indian Ocean.[32] This Australian reaction to the new U.S. Administration's ill-conceived initiative was especially sharp inasmuch as the larger ally had undertaken such discussions without even consulting Canberra. Since then, the Australians have made it absolutely clear to the United States that they consider the vast ocean which washes their western shores to be of crucial importance to them, and they expect to be consulted before any treaty ally moves to alter the status quo. Since the Australians feel so strongly about their national security stake in the Indian Ocean, they are accomplishing a major upgrading of the naval base at Cockburn Sound in southwestern Australia.

Reportedly, Canberra—despite manifest displeasure with the Carter move—has now made the base available for use by U.S. naval units en route to or operating in the Indian Ocean. Moreover, in September 1980, Defense Minister James Killen informed the Australian Parliament that American B-52 bombers would henceforth be permitted to use that country's airfields to facilitate extended flights into the Indian Ocean.[33]

The strategic import of this offer was almost immediately confirmed by actions of the Soviet Union. When the USSR's Ambassador in Canberra—Nikolai Soudirikov—learned about it, he immediately invited a group of Australian newspapermen to lunch where he proceeded to lobby against Frazer's initiative. In ham-handed fashion, he suggested that Canberra's move would inevitably render all of Australia a "nuclear target" for Soviet thermonuclear weapons.[34] Predictably, Prime Minister Frazer—widely known as a vociferous critic of the Soviet Union—denounced the Soviet Ambassador's intervention, including some very vitriolic comments about such a manner of conducting business between two governments. Moreover, he let it be understood that the Australian Government would proceed as planned and that such threats from the USSR would make no difference whatsoever. There can be little doubt that the Australians remain staunchly allied with the United States, Moscow's imprecations notwithstanding.

Finally, the Royal Australian Navy (RAN) is in a position to contribute to allied naval strength in the Indian Ocean. In a major speech on defense, Minister Killen further said that Australia would buy as many

---

[32]Hanks, "The Indian Ocean Negotiations . . ., *op. cit., p. 25*.
[33]"Australians Will Allow Landings by U.S. B-52s," *New York Times*, September 10, 1980, p. 14.
[34]Peter Costigan, "Soviet Envoy Criticizes Australia for Offering Base for U.S. Bombers," *Washington Star*, March 5, 1981, p. 26.

as six *Oliver Hazard Perry*-class frigates from the United States and would replace its aging aircraft carrier *Melbourne* with a new one capable of operating anti-submarine helicopters as well as the evolving vertical take-off and landing aircraft. In 1981, rumors circulated in the wake of major reductions announced for the Royal Navy that the Australians would buy one of the *Invincible*-class carriers London would be taking out of service or not completing. Whether this arrangement will go forward in light of the Argentinian seizure of the Falkland Islands in April 1982 is unknown. This action revealed the pitiful state to which the British Fleet has fallen and may well generate demands for shoring it up.

In the event of a true crisis in the Indian Ocean, one affecting Australia's vital interests, it can be reasonably assumed that elements of the RAN would be deployed to the hot spot. The validity of this assumption is attested to by the fact that, in October 1980, Australia provided visible evidence of its concern over the Iraq-Iran war. The carrier *Melbourne,* accompanied by at least three escorts and an oiler, transited the Indian Ocean to join the American, British and French naval forces cruising the waters of the Arabian Sea.[35]

The most populous nation in the Far East—the People's Republic of China—currently has very little in the way of military power which can reach beyond its own borders. Beijing, however, continues to flay the Soviets as the Sino-Soviet split endures. Constantly pointing to what it perceives as a single-minded Soviet drive for global hegemony," the new Chinese leadership continuously seeks to enlist the cooperation and assistance of other states to stem the projected Soviet campaign. In Beijing's view, current Soviet strategy encompasses a two-pronged drive for domination of all South Asia. One arm is seen directed through Iran and Pakistan toward the vital Persian Gulf. The other—primarily utilizing Vietnam, the "Cuba of the Far East," as a proxy—is aimed at control of Southeast Asia, particularly the Strait of Malacca. Since there is very little the Chinese themselves can currently do in the Indian Ocean region, they insist that their contribution to frustrating Moscow's ambitions lies in tying down some 46 Soviet divisions and a commensurate number of combat aircraft on their common border, teaching "lessons" to the Vietnamese surrogate, and delivering arms aid to Third World countries such as Pakistan.

Today, there are concerns within the security planning circles of the United States that the so-called opening to China may be unraveling. Current talks between Moscow and Beijing may be a harbinger of an ultimate rapprochement between the USSR and the PRC. Should this transpire, the change in the international power balance will be profound.

---

[35]Wilson, "Iraq-Bound Soviet Ships . . .," *op. cit.*

A major effect of such a change would be to exacerbate the strains which have been placed on the U.S. Navy by the expanded commitments in the Indian Ocean. It would be exceedingly difficult for the United States to maintain the current level of deployments to the Indian Ocean while restoring the strength of the Seventh Fleet in response to a Chinese shift toward Moscow. Only the future will tell whether such fears are valid, but in the meantime one must consider the signs ominous.

The Overall Outlook

On balance, it would appear that the United States will be forced, for the most part, to go it alone in the Indian Ocean and Persian Gulf regions in protecting its own and its allies' interests. Insofar as ground and air forces are concerned, assistance from extra-regional allies is highly unlikely. Thus, aside from naval support provided to date, and perhaps some help from West European nations and Japan in releasing U.S. forces from commitments to their defense, only the French, British and Australians appear to be in a position to make any sort of meaningful contribution.

Even for the British, however, the problem will be difficult in light of the decline which the Royal Navy and Royal Air Force have experienced in recent years. As noted, the confrontation with Argentina over the Falkland Islands highlighted the weakness of the British Fleet. Even *HMS Invincible*, flagship of the Royal Navy and of the squadron ordered to the South Atlantic in response to Argentina's seizure of the islands, was already destined to be sold to Australia as a replacement for the aging *Melbourne*. Moreover, the British Army presently has its hands more than full meeting its commitments on the continent of Europe while simultaneously coping with the bitter rebellion in Northern Ireland.

The French, on the other hand, have a significant military capability, including ground and naval forces stationed in the Indian Ocean. The problem here is essentially political in nature. It derives from the determined independence of Gaullist foreign policy which still exists and currently is being pursued just as assiduously by the government of François Mitterrand. As a matter of fact, to underline the fact that France can be expected to continue to follow an independent foreign policy, former French President Valery Giscard d'Estaing called for demilitarization of the Indian Ocean about the same time the United States was building up its naval forces in the region and announcing initial plans for the Rapid Deployment Joint Task Force. It is thus improbable that, barring a major regional disaster, the French will look favorably on any substantial overt cooperation with the United States.

12.
U.S. Policy Options

STEADY REDUCTIONS in American military power, which have transpired since the U.S. retreat from Vietnam, have severely limited the nation's ability to safeguard its interests. Nowhere is this fact more evident than in the Indian Ocean and Persian Gulf regions. Given the continuing political chaos in Iran, the Soviet invasion of Afghanistan, and the more recent Iraq-Iran war—where early 1982 successes by Iran threatened other oil-producing Persian Gulf states—it seems clear that Western interests in the area are being subjected to increasing jeopardy.

Here, perhaps, rests the foremost shortcoming of the North Atlantic Alliance. While this coalition may have been relevant to the immediate postwar threat posed by the Soviet Union, it is—given West European attitudes—clearly inadequate to the far wider, global challenges NATO faces today. The tragedy is that member states, by and large, refuse to do what is necessary to protect their own future. It is difficult in present circumstances to understand that posture. One suspects that the underlying factor is a belief on the part of West Europeans that, as with the defense of NATO, the United States will assume the bulk of the load elsewhere around the globe.

What they studiously ignore is the fact that the American people cannot be expected, forever, to bear a disproportionate burden of the common defense. The United States may, in the short term, be willing to carry an excessively large share of the load in defending Western Europe against Soviet aggression. Candor forces one to observe, however, that increasingly vocal trends to the contrary are now prevalent in the United States.

Understandably, Americans would likely maintain their traditional commitment—not necessarily in its present form—because they are generally convinced that domination of Western Europe by Moscow would inevitably shift the global balance of power to an extent that world dominion would finally be within the Kremlin's grasp. To avoid such a possibility, Americans are willing to make sacrifices on behalf of Western Europe, as they have proved by their support of NATO over the past three decades. Nonetheless, the economic pressures which afflict the United States in the early 1980s, coupled with the sacrifices its citizens are simultaneously being asked to make—primarily to resuscitate the U.S. armed forces—guarantee that they would take an exceedingly dim view of enduring those hardships in order to support allies who steadfastly refuse to emulate them.

The placing of American lives in jeopardy to preserve the flow of oil from the Persian Gulf *so long as that flow is crucial to the U.S. economy* would likewise be supported. But the notion that those lives would be put at risk to insure petroleum supplies primarily for Western Europe, particularly when Americans perceive that those nations are unwilling to contribute adequately to safeguard themselves, is simply not credible. It would be a serious mistake for such nations to think otherwise. Given the current strength of West European economies as compared with that of the United States, and the mood of the American people and their Congress, it is clear that the days when those nations could ride piggyback on the power of the U.S. armed forces are over.

Virtually the same thing can be said with respect to Japan. Here is another economy which owes much of its present strength to the American dollars which rebuilt it following World War II and then sustained its growth and modernization. This robust economy is also attributable to the Japanese Constitution—albeit imposed by the United States—prohibiting Tokyo from building and maintaining the kinds of military forces necessary to defend the country successfully. As a result, Japanese defense spending has been exceedingly low and the monies thus saved have played a major role in progressively modernizing and increasing the strength of the Japanese economy. Americans are well aware of this situation.

Whether individual nations such as Great Britain and France will actually cooperate with the United States when the need arises remains to be seen. One might look to major power conduct incident to the ongoing Iraq-Iran war for answers to this question. French and British actions to send warships to the vicinity of the threatened Strait of Hormuz, whether done as a result of close consultation with the United States or not, suggest that the prospects for Western cooperation in meeting challenges in the region have become somewhat more encouraging.

That U.S. policy options in the Middle East are severely constrained is manifest. Moreover, it is equally clear that the Arab states—moderate and radical alike—perceive the United States as the sole benefactor of their Zionist enemy: Israel. This is, perhaps, the single greatest barrier to the kind of cooperation Washington needs in the region. Thus, so long as the Arab-Israeli confrontation endures and the United States fails to exert sufficient political and economic pressure on Tel Aviv to produce the kinds of concessions without which a lasting peace is impossible, the attitude of Arab states in the Gulf area will remain essentially unchanged. With the exception of Oman, they will be reluctant to align themselves too closely with the United States.

There are developments, however, which could alter that situation. It has been said that there is nothing which focuses attention like an imminent hanging. Should the threat to the regional states posed by the Soviet Union be transformed into overt military aggression, either by the Soviets themselves or by Iraq or South Yemen acting in a surrogate capacity, the perceptions of the royal ruling families in the Gulf are likely to change dramatically. Moreover, should the Shiite regime in Iran emerge triumphant from its war with Iraq, and then turn its attention full time to the export of its fundamentalist revolutionary zeal throughout the Middle East, a similar change in the outlook of those states would surely follow.

For proof, one has only to look at Kuwait's panic-stricken reaction when Iraqi forces crossed the former's frontiers in 1973. Prior to that time, Kuwait had pursued a foreign policy characterized by an attempt to be friends with everyone and an ally of no one. Antagonisms were dealt with by buying off prospective predators, as in the case of Iraq, with oil revenues constituting the wherewithal. But that naive sort of foreign policy dissolved in the events of March 1973. As a result, Kuwait swiftly turned to the United States for military aid—weapons and training—with which to defend its borders. As for the threat from Iran, it is only necessary to recall the chill which gripped the shaikhdom of Bahrain when an Iranian plot to overthrow the al-Khalifa regime in December 1981 was uncovered just in time to thwart it. Thus, it is altogether likely that the states along the Persian Gulf littoral would quickly manifest an abrupt change in attitude in the event of a sudden, severe threat to their continued national existence, whatever the source.

The underlying problem, as with the present American military stance in the Indian Ocean, is that if one is aiming at deterrence—that is to say, to forestall aggressive moves—relevant action must be taken well in advance. This lesson seems to have escaped the Carter Administration. The vacillation of American foreign policy and the absence from the Indian Ocean region of relevant U.S. military strength contributed significantly to the political instability which began to infect nations in and around the Persian Gulf. Similarly, advance preparations—political and military—to protect the integrity of their borders must be taken by nations subject to aggressive assault, regardless of their geographic location. Recent Saudi Arabian fears that the Iraq-Iran war would spill over onto its territory—manifested by Riyadh's request for deployment of U.S. AWACS early-warning radar planes to the kingdom—reveal that the imminent hanging syndrome is not necessarily confined to threats emanating from the Soviet Union.

It beggars credibility to believe that the oil-producing states of the Persian Gulf are not acutely aware of the fact that, constituting one of the globe's two great "treasure houses," they are prime targets of those who seek to control the world. Thus, measures to adopt credible defensive postures and to cement those international relationships which offer promise of insuring their national independence should be the first order of business. That the Arabian Peninsula states have not turned to the United States for help—the one nation with sufficient military power to force caution on Soviet aggressive plans—can be ascribed directly to the pressures of the Arab-Israeli confrontation and the role the United States has played in that conflict.

In light of events in recent months, it would seem that the first order of business for Washington should be a dramatic increase in the size and capability of the American armed forces—particularly the U.S. Navy. After all, despite its continental dimensions, the United States is nevertheless an insular nation, one critically dependent upon unfettered use of the seas for its economic and military security. This is a basic truth which many Americans have forgotten. They have done so at their peril.

It is safe to say that the United States probably never has actually been independent of overseas sources of supplies. Regardless of the nature of the raw materials involved—petroleum, minerals or metals—this nation has always relied on supplies carried on the oceans, Alfred Thayer Mahan's "broad common," across which "ships sail to and fro." Today, the American problem is energy. Tomorrow, it will be the minerals and metals of the second great "store house," Southern Africa. Too few people in the United States realize that achievement of energy self-sufficiency would be to no avail if we do not have access to the materials with which that energy can be used to shape the finished output of a modern, industrial society.

The minerals and metals problem notwithstanding, a word must be said about the so-called global oil glut which appeared in the early 1980s. It is altogether true that dedicated conservation efforts, coupled with high prices, resulted in a sharply diminished world demand for petroleum during this period. An oversupply did indeed exist, but the duration of that happy circumstance is virtually impossible to forecast. It is true that resolution of the Iraq-Iran conflict could, in a reasonable time, restore these two major producers to full output, further adding to extant supplies. Finally, informed analysts are obviously correct when they assert that there remain vast reservoirs of crude oil around the world, yet to be discovered. Recent promising explorations in the Pacific Far East and off the West African Coast seemingly confirm their views.

On the other hand, it should be recognized that the United States and the rest of the Western world were, at the time the glut developed, in the throes of a serious recession—one bordering on economic depression. Manufacture of myriad commodities had been drastically curtailed and numerous plants had been completely shut down. Unemployment in the United States, for example, climbed to over 10 percent in the autumn of

1982. Many similar effects were being experienced in Western Europe and among the nations of the Pacific Far East.

Once this economic downturn is reversed and industrial output returns to normal or begins again to expand, demand for petroleum will most assuredly rise dramatically. Moreover, among nations of the Third World—where most of the globe's proven petroleum reserves are to be found—political instability, in one form or another, abounds. This situation is today particularly obvious in the Middle East, whether one is considering segments of the region east or west of Suez. It is only slightly less apparent with respect to Central Africa and northern South America.

Eruption of violence—domestic or external—in any one of a number of oil-producing nations could generate precisely the same sort of international energy crisis as that precipitated by the revolution in Iran or outbreak of war between that nation and Iraq. In short, the world petroleum balance continues to rest on a knife-edge, and it is patently susceptible to upset by even the most insignificant perturbation. Thus, complacency, such as that sired by the "oil glut," is the very last thing Western industrial nations should allow to cloud their views of the importance of the Middle East and its vast reserves of petroleum. Unless such an attitude is avoided, the oil abundance of the early 1980s could prove to be the siren call of the period, luring advanced industrial nations toward their downfall. Nor, before it is too late, should the metals and minerals situation be allowed to get out of hand.

Those who rule in the Kremlin are acutely aware of the West's critical dependence on the aforementioned "treasure houses" and are, today, exerting every effort to gain control of them. Should Moscow realize this objective, its ultimate goals would be achievable without the necessity for ordering a single Soviet soldier to cross the border into Western Europe. One is constrained to observe that this would constitute confirmation of the "indirect approach" theories of that eminent British strategist, Captain Sir Basil Liddell Hart.

Without relevant U.S. military power already stationed in or quickly deployable to the Indian Ocean-Persian Gulf region, there is no way any determined Soviet drive could be deterred or halted. Whether the Rapid Deployment Joint Task Force is the answer is an issue presently open to serious question. Furthermore, one can assume, with some degree of certainty, that the ultimate Force—even as envisioned—would not really be applicable to the most prevalent threats likely to erupt in and around the Persian Gulf. The recent Iraq-Iran war abundantly demonstrated the validity of this assertion. By and large, these sorts of crises will be relatively minor, far less intense than the kind requiring the power represented in the projected Rapid Deployment Joint Task Force.

The basic U.S. dilemma therefore centers on other alternatives. The first which comes to mind is the amphibious capability of the United States Navy-Marine Corps team. Over the years, this is the arm of the American military Washington has most frequently called upon to put things right wherever in the world they have gone wrong for the United States. Why not the same approach to future crises in the Indian Ocean-Persian Gulf region?

For decades the quick-reaction capability of the United States military has been exemplified by the U.S. Marine Corps. Transported to the troubled area in nearby-deployed naval amphibious shipping, the Marines have habitually landed in hot spots shortly after a crisis erupted. The pertinent point is that the Marines, while seldom present in overwhelming numbers, invariably have arrived on the scene first. Lebanon in 1958, the Dominican Republic in 1965, and elsewhere, the U.S. Marine Corps— with its amphibious landing expertise and rapid reaction capability—has been able to snuff out incipient crises before they have become full-blown international catastrophes. This, it would appear, is exactly what is needed to meet the most likely threats in the Middle East.

To be sure, the threat posed by the USSR cannot be ignored. Given the close proximity of Soviet military power and the incredibly long distance any American forces would have to travel, it seems obvious that any response to an overt Soviet incursion in the Middle East, on the Afghanistan pattern, would have to be multinational in character. Moreover, it should be, if for no other reason than the fact that Soviet domination of the region's petroleum supplies is unquestionably an international problem.

While the United States should assuredly press ahead with development of the Rapid Deployment Joint Task Force, along with prepositioning sizable amounts of proper military equipment in proximity to potential crisis points, Washington should simultaneously be working assiduously to form a latter-day *entente cordiale,* one enlisting the cooperation of selected countries—regional and extra-regional—to present a solid international front to Soviet expansionism in the Persian Gulf-Indian Ocean area. The nations of the region should be encouraged to construct a meaningful defensive alliance aimed at safeguarding, to the best of their collective abilities, their own frontiers. A larger and more powerful external entente—promoted by the United States—should be pledged to step in with whatever additional military power might be necessary to augment local efforts in deterring Soviet advances, or defeating them should deterrence fail. In this regard, it should be noted that such an international grouping would be in a position to threaten retaliation against Soviet vital interests elsewhere around the globe wherever they might prove to be vulnerable. As any competent strategist knows, it is always exceedingly foolish to accept conflict exclusively on an adversary's terms. Nowhere is this more true than in the Middle East.

U.S. interests are global in nature in the closing years of the twentieth century. The country's overall national strategy begs for recognition of this modern-day reality. An insular nation, despite its continental scope, the United States must devise a strategy that is maritime in nature. Recent developments in the Indian Ocean-Persian Gulf region underline this thesis. It seems evident that the Reagan Administration accepts this national security argument. The naval shipbuilding program featured in the 1983 U.S. Defense Department budget supports such an assertion. The Middle East and its problems are indicative of the broader challenges which the United States must address if its security is to be assured.

As for the Middle East, major improvements in the U.S. military posture in that critical region are mandatory if the American international voice is not only to be heard, but heeded. It is fair to say that the welfare of the United States, Western Europe and Japan as well as that of moderate Arab regimes in and around the Persian Gulf—whether or not the latter believe it—depends heavily on the power of that voice.

Appendix

FY 1983-87 Shipbuilding Program

Type of Ship	82[1]	83	84	85	86	87	FY 83-87 Five Year Total
TRIDENT (Ballistic Missile Submarine)	—	2	1	1	1	1	6
SSN-688 (Attack Submarine)	2	2	3	4	4	4	17
CVN (Aircraft Carrier-Nuclear)	—	2	—	—	—	—	2
CV (Aircraft Carrier) SLEP[2]	—	1	—	1	—	1	3
CG-47 (Guided Missile Cruiser)	3	3	3	3	4	4	17
CG-42 (Nuclear Guided Missile Cruiser)	—	—	—	—	—	1	1
DDG-51 (Guided Missile Destroyer)	—	—	—	1	—	3	4
DD (Destroyer)	—	—	—	—	2	1	3
BB (Battleship) Reactivation	1	1	1	1	—	—	3
FFG-7 (Guided Missile Frigate)	3	2	2	2	3	3	12
MCM (Mine Countermeasure Ship)	1	4	4	5	—	—	13
MSH (Mine Countermeasure Ship)	—	—	1	—	5	5	11
LSD-41 (Landing Ship Dock)	1	1	1	2	2	2	8
LHD-1 (Amphibious Ship)	—	—	1	—	—	1	2
AOE (Multi-Purpose Stores Ship)	—	—	—	1	1	2	4
AE (Ammunition Ship)	—	—	—	1	2	1	4
ARS (Salvage Ship)	2	1	1	—	—	—	2
AD (Destroyer Tender)	—	—	—	—	1	1	2
T-AO (Oiler)	1	1	3	4	4	6	18
T-AGS (FBM Support Ship) Conversion	—	—	—	2	—	—	2
T-AK (Cargo Ship) Conversion	—	—	—	1	—	—	1
T-ARC (Cable Ship)	—	—	—	—	1	—	1
T-AGM (Range Instrumentation Ship) Conversion	—	—	—	—	1	—	1
T-AGOS/AGOS (SURTASS)	4	—	1	—	2	3	6
T-AKRX (SL-7) Conversion[3]	4	4	—	—	—	—	4
T-AFS (Stores Ship) Conversion	2	—	—	—	—	—	0
T-AH (Conversion)	—	1	1	—	—	—	2
New Construction Ships	17	18	21	24	32	38	133
Conversions/SLEPS/Reactivations	7	7	2	5	1	1	16

[1]Shown for information to reflect changed baseline from Carter program.
[2]SLEP—Service Life Extension Program.
[3]Acquisition of eight T-AKRXs will be completed in FY 1982.

Source: Caspar W. Weinburger, *Annual Report to the Congress, Fiscal Year 1983*, p. III-36.

INSTITUTE FOR FOREIGN POLICY ANALYSIS, INC.
List of Publications

Foreign Policy Reports

DEFENSE TECHNOLOGY AND THE ATLANTIC ALLIANCE: COMPETITION OR COLLABORATION? By Frank T. J. Bray and Michael Moodie. April 1977. 42pp. $5.00.

IRAN'S QUEST FOR SECURITY: U.S. ARMS TRANSFERS AND THE NUCLEAR OPTION. By Alvin J. Cottrell and James E. Dougherty. May 1977. 59pp. $5.00.

ETHIOPIA, THE HORN OF AFRICA, AND U.S. POLICY. By John H. Spencer. September 1977. 69pp. $5.00. (Out of print.)

BEYOND THE ARAB-ISRAELI SETTLEMENT: NEW DIRECTIONS FOR U.S. POLICY IN THE MIDDLE EAST. By R. K. Ramazani. September 1977. 69pp. $5.00.

SPAIN, THE MONARCHY AND THE ATLANTIC COMMUNITY. By David C. Jordan. June 1979. 55pp. $5.00.

U.S. STRATEGY AT THE CROSSROADS: TWO VIEWS. By Robert J. Hanks and Jeffrey Record. July 1982. 69 pp. $7.50.

Special Reports

The papers in this series of Special Reports on Foreign Policy and National Security are addressed to current and emerging issues of critical importance and published on a "quick-reaction" basis. This series contains sufficient scope for treatment of all major issue areas of U.S. foreign policy and world affairs.

THE CRUISE MISSILE: BARGAINING CHIP OR DEFENSE BARGAIN? By Robert L. Pfaltzgraff, Jr., and Jacquelyn K. Davis. January 1977. x, 53pp. $3.00.

EUROCOMMUNISM AND THE ATLANTIC ALLIANCE. By James E. Dougherty and Diane K. Pfaltzgraff. January 1977. xiv, 66pp. $3.00.

THE NEUTRON BOMB: POLITICAL, TECHNICAL AND MILITARY ISSUES. By S. T. Cohen. November 1978. xii, 95pp. $6.50.

SALT II AND U.S. STRATEGIC FORCES. By Jacquelyn K. Davis, Patrick J. Friel and Robert L. Pfaltzgraff, Jr. June 1979. xii, 51pp. $5.00.

THE EMERGING STRATEGIC ENVIRONMENT: IMPLICATIONS FOR BALLISTIC MISSILE DEFENSE. By Leon Gouré, William G. Hyland and Colin S. Gray. December 1979. xi, 75pp. $6.50.

THE SOVIET UNION AND BALLISTIC MISSILE DEFENSE. By Jacquelyn K. Davis, Uri Ra'anan, Robert L. Pfaltzgraff, Jr., Michael J. Deane and John M. Collins. March 1980. xi, 71pp. $6.50. (Out of print.)

ENERGY ISSUES AND ALLIANCE RELATIONSHIPS: THE UNITED STATES, WESTERN EUROPE AND JAPAN. By Robert L. Pfaltzgraff, Jr. April 1980. xii, 71pp. $6.50.

U.S. STRATEGIC-NUCLEAR POLICY AND BALLISTIC MISSILE DEFENSE: THE 1980S AND BEYOND. By William Schneider, Jr., Donald G. Brennan, William A. Davis, Jr., and Hans Rühle. April 1980. xii, 61pp. $6.50.

THE UNNOTICED CHALLENGE: SOVIET MARITIME STRATEGY AND THE GLOBAL CHOKE POINTS. By Robert J. Hanks. August 1980. xi, 66pp. $6.50.

FORCE REDUCTIONS IN EUROPE: STARTING OVER. By Jeffrey Record. October 1980. xi, 92pp. $6.50.

SALT II AND AMERICAN SECURITY. By Gordon J. Humphrey, William R. Van Cleave, Jeffrey Record, William H. Kincade, and Richard Perle. October 1980. xvi, 65 pp.

THE FUTURE OF U.S. LAND-BASED STRATEGIC FORCES. By Jake Garn, J. I. Coffey, Lord Chalfont, and Ellery B. Block. December 1980. xvi, 80pp.

THE CAPE ROUTE: IMPERILED WESTERN LIFELINE. By Robert J. Hanks. February 1981. xi, 80pp. $6.50 (Hardcover, $10.00).

THE RAPID DEPLOYMENT FORCE AND U.S. MILITARY INTERVENTION IN THE PERSIAN GULF. By Jeffrey Record. February 1981. viii, 82pp. $7.50 (Hardcover, $12.00).

POWER PROJECTION AND THE LONG-RANGE COMBAT AIRCRAFT: MISSIONS, CAPABILITIES, AND ALTERNATIVE DESIGNS. By Jacquelyn K. Davis and Robert L. Pfaltzgraff, Jr. June 1981. ix, 37 pp. $6.50.

THE PACIFIC FAR EAST: ENDANGERED AMERICAN STRATEGIC POSITION. By Robert J. Hanks. October 1981. ix, 75pp. $7.50.

NATO'S THEATER NUCLEAR FORCE MODERNIZATION PROGRAM: THE REAL ISSUES. By Jeffrey Record. November 1981. vii, 102pp. $7.50.

THE CHEMISTRY OF DEFEAT: ASYMMETRIES IN U.S. AND SOVIET CHEMICAL WARFARE POSTURES. By Amoretta M. Hoeber. December 1981. xiii, 91pp. $6.50.

THE HORN OF AFRICA: A MAP OF POLITICAL-STRATEGIC CONFLICT. By James E. Dougherty. April 1982. xv, 74pp. $7.50.

THE WEST, JAPAN AND CAPE ROUTE IMPORTS: THE OIL AND NON-FUEL MINERAL TRADES. By Charles Perry. June 1982. xiv, 88pp. $7.50.

Books

ATLANTIC COMMUNITY IN CRISIS: A REDEFINITION OF THE ATLANTIC RELATIONSHIP. Edited by Walter F. Hahn and Robert L. Pfaltzgraff, Jr. Pergamon Press, 1979. 386pp. $43.00.

SOVIET MILITARY STRATEGY IN EUROPE. By Joseph D. Douglass, Jr. Pergamon Press, 1980. 252pp. $33.00.

THE WARSAW PACT: ARMS, DOCTRINE, AND STRATEGY. By William J. Lewis. New York: McGraw-Hill Publishing Co., 1982. 471pp. $29.95.

Conference Reports

NATO AND ITS FUTURE: A GERMAN-AMERICAN ROUNDTABLE. Summary of a Dialogue. 1978. 22pp. $1.00.

SECOND GERMAN-AMERICAN ROUNDTABLE ON NATO: THE THEATER-NUCLEAR BALANCE. A Conference Report. 1978. 32pp. $1.00.

THE SOVIET UNION AND BALLISTIC MISSILE DEFENSE. A Conference Report. 1978. 26pp. $1.00.

U.S. STRATEGIC-NUCLEAR POLICY AND BALLISTIC MISSILE DEFENSE: THE 1980S AND BEYOND. A Conference Report. 1979. 30pp. $1.00.

SALT II AND AMERICAN SECURITY. A Conference Report. 1979. 39pp.

THE FUTURE OF U.S. LAND-BASED STRATEGIC FORCES. A Conference Report. 1979. 32pp.

THE FUTURE OF NUCLEAR POWER. A Conference Report. 1980. 48pp. $1.00.

THIRD GERMAN-AMERICAN ROUNDTABLE ON NATO: MUTUAL AND BALANCED FORCE REDUCTIONS IN EUROPE: A Conference Report. 1980. 27pp. $1.00.

79

FOURTH GERMAN-AMERICAN ROUNDTABLE ON NATO: NATO MODERNIZATION AND EUROPEAN SECURITY. A Conference Report. 1981. 15pp. $1.00.

SECOND ANGLO-AMERICAN SYMPOSIUM ON DETERRENCE AND EUROPEAN SECURITY. A Conference Report. 1981. 25pp. $1.00.

THE U.S. DEFENSE MOBILIZATION INFRASTRUCTURE: PROBLEMS AND PRIORITIES. A Conference Report (The Tenth Annual Conference, sponsored by the International Security Studies Program, The Fletcher School of Law and Diplomacy, Tufts University). 1981. 25pp. $1.00.

U.S. STRATEGIC DOCTRINE FOR THE 1980S. A Conference Report. 1982. 14pp.

FRENCH-AMERICAN SYMPOSIUM ON STRATEGY, DETERRENCE AND EUROPEAN SECURITY. A Conference Report. 1982. 14pp. $1.00.

FIFTH GERMAN-AMERICAN ROUNDTABLE ON NATO: THE CHANGING CONTEXT OF THE EUROPEAN SECURITY DEBATE. Summary of a Transatlantic Dialogue. A Conference Report. 1982. 22 pp. $1.00.

ENERGY SECURITY AND THE FUTURE OF NUCLEAR POWER. A Conference Report. 1982. 39pp. $2.50.

INTERNATIONAL SECURITY DIMENSIONS OF SPACE. A Conference Report (The Eleventh Annual Conference, sponsored by the International Security Studies Program, The Fletcher School of Law and Diplomacy, Tufts University). 1982. 24pp. $2.50.